Life *in the* Slow Lane

THE WORLD AROUND ME AND ME

DAVID MORRISON

Ark House Press
arkhousepress.com

© 2025 David Morrison

All rights reserved. Apart from any fair dealing for the purpose of study, research, criticism, or review, as permitted under the Copyright Act, no part may be reproduced by any process without written permission.

Cataloguing in Publication Data:
Title: Life in the Slow Lane
ISBN: 978-1-7642308-8-9 (pbk)
Subjects: REL012170 RELIGION / Christian Living / Personal Memoirs; BIO018000 BIOGRAPHY & AUTOBIOGRAPHY / Religious; BIO026000   BIOGRAPHY & AUTOBIOGRAPHY / Memoirs.

Design by initiateagency.com

The Goodooga Post Office and Postmaster's residence in 1961

Contents

Preface	1
Introduction	3
Pre-marriage Family	7
Life in Wahroonga- or Home and Away	11
A Cousin	15
Someone Else	16
Ancestral Musings	17
Politics	19
Sitting in the Gallery	23
Writing letters	26
Education	27
A Job or Two	28
Christian Work	32
Life in Goodooga	34
On the Way to Goodooga	36
Sydney Morrison Once More	38
The Sister	40
Music	41
Thoughts (mine)	43
No traveller	48
Christian Thinking	49
Marriage	51
Springwood	53
A Vegetarian's Lament	54
Teaching Geography	57
Another Snake Story- at the Picture Show	60
Dry Cleaning	62
Change and Mud	63

The Local Baker	66
Church Music Once More	68
Spoonerisms	72
Tiddles and…	74
…the bag	75
Prime Ministers	76
Letters to Newspapers and Magazines- the Detail	78
Letters to *The Blue Mountains Gazette*	81
The Verandah	86
Letters to *The Sydney Morning Herald*	88
Some Interesting People	94
Examinations on a Sunday	96
An Old Soldier and Others	97
John Cowland	99
Letter about John Cowland	100
Letters to *The Australian*	102
English usage	110
Genuine Composition	112
Time to Eat	114
Flora and fauna	116
Fashion	117
Back to the early years Fire!!	119
Colours	120
People I have observed	122
Fireworks	129
Letters again. (How many more, you ask?!)	131
Auntie Margaret and the DC3	142
Teaching Music	143
The Manly Ferry	145
Look whom they're accepting now!	148
Batteries for sitting on	149

Uncle Joe and Auntie Flo	151
A Bird at Goodooga	154
Papyrus and Adolf Deissman	156
The Patons	158
My Pruen Connection with Edward Jenner, *or*	
Sir Henry Parkes meets Grandma, *or* Avuncular Vaccinations	159
The Photography Exhibition and the Talent Quest	161
The Old Hotel at Dubbo	163
George Henry	165
The First Fleet	167
Some Family Detail from Uncle Charlie	168
The Mass Media	170
Left Almost Alone in the Exam Room	173
Anaesthetics	174
Paper! Paper!	175
So Young	177
School Discipline in days of yore	178
The Milkman	180
The Baker	181
The Village Store	182
Ice	184
Mother's Day	186
Freedom	187
Petticoat Government	190
Never Fear	191
Pulpits of sand	192
A Trip not Taken	194
The Elephant not in the Room	195
Sir Owen Dixon	196
Blackboards	197
Final Anecdotes	199

Preface

This book has been in the process of composition in my mind for decades. It seemed about time to collect the notes I had made over the years and put them into some sort of form that would make a reasonably easy to read account of my "take" on the things that have happened in my lifetime, or in a few cases, before it. My main reason for writing these pages is to provide something for our extended family to read, but a wider audience may well find some interest in it. Some coverage has been given to my side of family history so that the people after our generation may have an idea of who has gone before and perhaps an inkling or two of how they have affected those who have followed them.

Over the years I have from time to time told children and grandchildren and others various things about family history, but different things have been told to different ones and much of what has been told would be forgotten anyway. Bits of the family story being dropped in as the book proceeds is one way of ensuring that at least some salient facts and observations are preserved in some form for future family readers. There is much information about the family in our cupboards and files, including family trees, historical information and photographs. On the assumption that such material will be still extant after my generation's departure it will be possible for family members to study it if at any time they are interested to do so. Perhaps this book may even whet the appetite of some keen family historian!

Introduction

You beat your pate, and fancy wit will come:
Knock as you please, there's nobody at home.

Alexander Pope (1688-1744)

Most writers, great and small, waiting for inspiration will feel the force of Pope's couplet- a clever poem in miniature. Pope there fulfils his own observation that some can write about something in a way "as oft was thought, but ne'er so well expressed". At my age even keeping things together in the head in order to bring them to the page in some sort of order is hard enough, let alone trying to express them in a clear, well-written way. But enough of Pope, who was before my time. Some may choose to begin their literary judgement by wondering how such a grammatical pedant could have chosen the subtitle for this book. Feel free to ponder!

As I said in the Preface, my purpose in writing these stories is to set down some thoughts about the events that have occurred during my lifetime- eighty-six years so far- including events that have shaped the world down to those that in particular have shaped me. The quotation from Pope is my excuse for not being as mentally agile or inspired as one would hope to be when putting things into writing and hoping they will survive the test of time, even a relatively short time. This is less an autobiography than it is a collection of stories about family and observations on material based on the years since I first became aware of the big world around me.

In fact it's not so much a scintillating chronology as a prosaic mosaic. Some of my thoughts about various matters will have a chronological sequence, with headings, but some will be "all over the place", maybe with headings and maybe not. Rather than having a section of interesting and perhaps amusing anecdotes in one place, or as they occur in particular tales, there will be little interludes here and there with what I hope may keep the interest slightly piqued. The main intended readers are the descendants of Anna and me, plus perhaps some other relatives and acquaintances, but I have no objection to as wide a readership as possible. I will leave the translation into other languages to those more able than I. (Note that pedantic grammar!)

The precise details of dates, direct quotations and so on may suffer from the vagaries of aging memory, but I hope the substance is correct and that small errors will be forgiven- if a reader happens to notice them. Somewhere I was reading about so-called "fictitious biographies", a term not always referring to biographies of fictitious people. I suppose all biographies are partly fictitious and the temptation to be liberal with the facts is especially strong with an autobiography or a work with autobiographical material in it. I'm certainly not going to relate all my perceived failings or embarrassing moments. Don't say "Oh!". I'm just not.

During the eighty or more years covered by my memory the world has of course seen some very big changes, many of which are well-known and well-documented. Other changes have not been known outside their immediate locale while they were occurring and of course many factors such as the continuous "turnover" of people caused by births and deaths is causing constant change. It is interesting to ponder the fact that an individual can know only an infinitesimal amount of what goes on in the world each day, let alone back through history. Even a historian or historiographer who seems to know a great deal really knows very little of what happened in the past.

What they do know and can tell us and evaluate is of course very useful in helping us understand the present world in the light of the past. What we know at present about most of the people in our own street may be slight, let alone knowledge of mankind at large. Some people in some places have barely a nodding acquaintance with their next-door neighbours. That's not good.

One exercise I used to give my geography students involved looking at a topographical map with imagination. Those maps of course are large-scale and cover only a small area, maybe five kilometres square (not to be confused with five square kilometres, which is one-fifth that area) or less. They show the main fixed natural and human features in the area including roads and, in some cases, individual buildings. The students were asked to think of a time of day and a day of the week and imagine the movements of people in the mapped area. That would include vehicle movements, people walking dogs and possibly many other details. There was a lot more to it than that, but the point for our purposes here is to help us remember that a huge amount of human activity may be going on in a small area, perhaps quite close to us, that we can know about only in a broad sense, if at all.

A speck in space- Therefore, what follows is the product of a tiny speck of grey matter in a vast world in a vast solar system…you get the idea. Many of us look back with nostalgia to various aspects of earlier days. That is natural and has always been so. Our backward-looking spectacles are sometimes rather rose-tinted and as well as remembering mostly the good things we can also exaggerate the difficulties of the past. Years ago I read in Readers' Digest (I think it was there) how looking back changes with the generations. When I was very young older people used to tell me how far they used to walk to get to school. The magazine said that nowadays people tend to say "Don't complain! I had to drive to school without power steering". At the time of writing this I expect it may soon be "I had to drive with a steering wheel" or without the help of AI.

Nostalgia can confuse our thinking at times. After my father died one of his cousins told me of one of his sayings- "Things are not as they were. In fact, they never were." Some even say that nostalgia isn't what it used to be. Most of the words that follow will apply to the years of my lifetime. There will be a bit of looking back to earlier times where it seems appropriate.

Pre-marriage Family

Unlike some biographies and autobiographies (which this is not anyway) the reader will not have to endure a catalogue of how my great-great-grandfather studied Latin at Oxford (and I would be very surprised to find that he had) or my great-grandmother's adeptness at milking cows (a more likely possibility). We'll stick mainly to the two parents and two grandparents that I remember and who affected my life in some way, but Grandpa and Grandma will not loom large. Some other relatives will be mentioned here and there in the book.

My parents were Sydney and Thelma Morrison. They were married in 1935 and at the time I was born were living in Burns Road, Wahroonga, a northern suburb of Sydney. I always find biographies a bit tedious when they go back in detail for several generations before getting to the life of the subject. The same could be said of hybrid ramblings such as this composition. Where various forbears and other relatives happen to be relevant to any of my stories they will find their place in the appropriate location. The primary natal fact is that I was born in March, 1939, meaning that I can claim to be a pre-war baby.

My brother Robert, my sister Wendy and I were born at Roslyn Hospital in Lindfield, a northern suburb of Sydney, some kilometres south of Wahroonga. I remember visiting my mother in hospital when I was two and a half and seeing babies through a window. I don't remember what I *thought* it was all about, but it was indeed about Wendy, my newly born baby sister. My next early memory is one of going by train to Canberra when I was just three, but my only memories of the occasion are the white train and the front yard of the house where we stayed. The house, close to the original Parliament House, belonged to, or was rented by, Harold and Margery Wickett, Marjorie being a first cousin of my mother.

My father, Sydney Morrison, served as a lance-corporal in the army in the First World War until he was badly wounded and discharged on a small life pension. More will be said later about his war service. After the war he rejected any further pension payments, went back to work and was able to enlist again for the Second World War, this time to serve in Australia. He practised with the artillery in Queensland while there was fear of a Japanese invasion and later he was a guard at the prisoner-of-war camp in Cowra, a town in inland southern New South Wales.

My mother, Thelma, could see that her husband was "chaffing at the bit" and she encouraged him to enlist for the second major war of the era. He did so on 17th March, 1942 and was discharged on 16th July, 1945, after the

European victory but a few weeks before the capitulation of Japan. As with so many other women at the time, his absence left my mother with the care of us three children, but to her advantage (and sometimes disadvantage) my father's three unmarried sisters lived next door. We three children of course came to know the "Three Aunts" very well and they loved us and we loved them. On some rare occasions they took us in hand if we didn't live up to their expectations. They were after all three strict Presbyterian ladies, Cath, Flora and Milly (or was it Millie?).

My parents kept me back from school until I was nearly six. The reasons were my frequent illnesses and what they must have perceived as my "delicate condition". Unlike my brother and sister, I didn't attend any pre-school. Although I was late learning to read and write (I couldn't read well until I was nine) the home atmosphere was very conducive to learning general knowledge and what might be called preparation for reading. Once the reading began to flow at age nine I was always one of the better readers in my school classes (which wasn't all that remarkable as I look back at some of my fellow-pupils). Relatives and others who visited our home often engaged with my parents in interesting conversations about politics and other subjects. I usually listened in with avid attention, whether I understood what was said or not.

Some of my impressions of the last year or so of the war are connected with the radio. That was the "wireless set" on the shelf. One tedious time of the day was 12:30 PM when the ABC news was scheduled on the radio. I was required to keep quiet for fifteen minutes while my mother listened. I remember at one stage thinking that it must be almost compulsory to begin the news with the words "Allied troops…". I think my mother must have told me that the term applied in its wider sense to "soldiers, sailors and airmen". I do remember clearly that she encouraged me to pray for those three groups of (mainly) men.

My first letter to a newspaper was at about the age of twelve. I remember including the words "this corrupt government" and I remember my father advising me not to send it since I might be sued for libel! I capitulated and the letter was not sent! The image of a twelve-year-old standing in court being cross-examined by a leading silk must have been more than I could bear.

Life in Wahroonga- or Home and Away

My first few years of school were interrupted by illness. In 1947 at the age of eight scarlet fever stopped me in my tracks for six weeks. An ambulance took my mother and me to the Prince Henry Hospital at Little Bay, a suburban area south of the Sydney CBD. My mother had not dressed for a trip home through the city by tram and train, but I think she did at least have her handbag and was able to pay the fares. The hospital had an isolation ward which became my home for three weeks.

My parents were permitted to visit me once a week, talking through a window from the corridor. My brother and sister loved the incident because they were required to stay home from school in isolation for a few days until it was clear they were not infected. There were another three weeks of convalescence at home. It was not long after that that penicillin was used to treat patients with scarlet fever and the recovery time was greatly reduced. That first stay in hospital was outplayed by my next one.

In 1949 the doctor noticed a funny heartbeat. Did I say "funny"? About twenty years a later another doctor actually began to giggle as he listened to my heart beating in an irregular way. But back to the story. The 1949 doctor diagnosed me with a serious infection, it being probably caused by a streptococcal bacterium. A small private hospital beckoned, Dalcross Hospital in Killara, and while the penicillin injections stopped after three five-day courses my stay extended to eight weeks. It was decided that I wouldn't lose the infection unless my tonsils were removed.

The problem was that a tonsil operation was a risk while I still had the infection! They sent me home for Christmas and in January I was admitted to Hornsby District Hospital where my operation was attended by a specialist anaesthetist and a specialist surgeon. The operation was observed by my GP and a neighbour who just happened to be a heart specialist. I lived on. Dear Auntie Cath paid the big gap payment for my long stay at Dalcross.

Most of my first thirty-two years were lived in Wahroonga. In some ways it was almost rural when my parents moved there in about 1935 but by the time I left and married at the end of 1971 it had become very urban, if still a leafy and quiet place. Two doors from us lived Sir Lionel Lindsay, one of Norman Lindsay's brothers and a good friend of Sir Robert Menzies who was for over sixteen continuous years Prime Minister of Australia. It was always a thrill for us Morrison children to see the big black car arrive and to see Sir Robert and Dame Pattie, his wife, step out and go in to visit Sir Lionel and Lady Lindsay. Sir Lionel once told my father that he was at an airport with Menzies and they spied the Leader of the Federal Opposition, Dr Bert Evatt. Sir Lionel commented that Dr Evatt didn't look very well and Menzies replied "Don't say that. He's my greatest asset!"

Some of my childhood and early teenage memories include my uncle, Clive Bayliss, my mother's brother, when he returned after some years in a Japanese prison camp in Kuching, Borneo, in what is now Malaysia. His wife, Auntie Lorna to us, had lived for a time with her son Paul in Cowra, away from the perceived dangers of a coastal invasion, the same town where my father served as a prison guard in the latter part of the war. They had moved inland to avoid the danger of being on the coast when and if the Japanese invaded, but when the danger was well and truly past they came to live with us in our small three-bedroom house in Wahroonga until Clive returned. He finally arrived back in the hospital ship *Wanganella* in either December 1945 or January 1946. Some of the extended family travelled on a Manly ferry in order to see the ship anchored just inside the Sydney Heads and we held up a big banner with "Clive Bayliss" on it. He didn't see it. I mention this again in my observations on Sydney ferries.

The family didn't know at the time how the order from Tokyo to kill all prisoners was rescinded at the last minute. Clive lived with us for a while after he returned and told us then and over the following years some interesting stories about his time in the prison camp. He and his fellow prisoners were treated better than prisoners in most such camps and it was only after his death that I learned from a book that the wife of the Japanese commandant was a Christian lady. Perhaps the commandant was a Christian too. He unfortunately decided in traditional fashion that the only thing to do at the end was to fall on his sword.

> When I was teaching at St Ives North primary school in the 1960s I had in my Fourth Class (Year 4 these days) a Japanese

boy who was in Australia while his father worked here for a time. During a craft lesson with the boys in the class, a good time for chatting about things and building rapport man and boy, he told me that his father had been a suicide pilot during the war. When I queried how his father could still be alive in the 1960s, he said that the night before his group was to take off and crash into American warships the Americans flew over the airfield and bombed it to the point where the fighter planes were unable to take off the next morning. That was a close shave! Thinking that perhaps his father had been very disappointed at not being able to give his life in that way for his country, I asked Yasukuni what his father thought about the American raid. His reply was an enthusiastic "Oh! Phew Sir!".

A Cousin

Paul Bayliss and I were born six months apart, Paul being born a few weeks after the war with Germany had started and my birthday being six months before the war. We went to Waitara Public School together while he was staying with us and, even though older than I was, he was in First Class (Year One) while I was in Kindergarten. When we were around the ages of eleven to thirteen we stayed at one another's homes at times and sometimes went on Saturday afternoon (very tame) adventures. We were always good friends as well as cousins and although, once we were married, our meetings were few and far between we have remained good friends into our eighties. One memory is of our maiden aunt, Muriel Bayliss, and Paul's maiden aunt, "Biddie" Walkden-Brown, taking us to the Sydney Royal Easter Show, until we were old enough to go unsupervised by adults. My favourite show attractions in those days were the ghost train and the "wall of death" where a motorcyclist drove his bike around the inside of a hollow cylinder while spectators watched from above.

Someone Else

I must not forget Mr Rofe. He lived not far from us and at one stage I used to meet his grandson in the morning and we would walk to school, sometimes with my brother Robert and Paul Bayliss. When I was quite young Mr Rofe saw me in the train with my parents and gave me what was known a "half-penny" coin (pronounced *hape-nee*). His generosity was not so great since he was a millionaire in the days when a million pounds was a lot of money. An inflation calculator tells me that in 2025 value in it would be well over eighty million dollars. Compared to Australia's billionaires today it would of course be only spare cash.

> When I lived and taught in Goodooga (which you will hear about again) we had a carols by candle light evening in the local hall. In the days before daylight saving it was quite dark by 8:00 PM, that being as far as I recall the time of the event. I was seated at the piano ready to play the first carol and all the people in the hall with candles lit them. The carol was announced, I began to read the music and as I started to play, the electric lights went out. Someone hastily found some sort of lamp and I then had just enough light to see the music and resume playing.

Ancestral Musings

I could start with a silly pun about the story of the three bears as I begin to talk about three of our forebears. But none of that. It may interest family members- children, grandchildren, great-grandchildren and so on to know or be reminded of three prominent people from whom they are descended. On my father's Morrison side it has been alleged that we are descended from the great Scottish Protestant Reformer, John Knox. He was born in about 1514 and died in 1572. He was what is known as a Calvinist (as a majority of Protestants were then) and had some influence on the development of the English Books of Common Prayer.

He was reputedly a powerful preacher who could talk at great length. It is said that Mary Queen of Scots, a Roman Catholic lady, claimed that she trembled when John Knox prayed. As well as reforming Christian belief and practice John Knox did some other things with good results, including the formation of the Scottish education system which was separate from England's and which became renowned for its high quality for centuries afterwards.

Another supposed forbear on my mother's side was Lord Harley, Earl of Oxford. He served in the House of Commons in the British Parliament and when his father died he inherited the title and moved to the House of Lords. He lived on this earth from 1661 to 1724. Several of our family members have had the middle name "Harley", including the person writing this book. When I was a boy I was told that someday we might all inherit part of the "Harley

Millions", perhaps billions in today's values, but we are all still waiting. Having the name doesn't seem to have worked- so far. Take note, family.

The third name that comes to mind is that of Edward Jenner, the man who did the most to develop a good vaccination for smallpox. On my mother's side he is our great-great-great… uncle. So we are not actually descended from him, but maybe close enough. The world is very thankful for a great reduction in deaths and disfigurement from smallpox, but I have a bone to pick with him. When I had a smallpox vaccination at about thirty years of age I was confined to bed for several days, very sick with vaccinia (a severe reaction to vaccination).

Politics

My interest in politics began early, mostly no doubt because, as mentioned earlier, the adults around me frequently discussed the issues of the day, including the actions of politicians in and out of government. My first memory of actually listening to political speeches on the radio was in about 1951 when the Prime Minister, Mr (later Sir Robert) Menzies, spoke to audiences in halls and the ABC broadcast them as they were happening ("live", as we say now). I remember pre-election speeches in 1954 by Dr Evatt, the Labor leader, and the leader of the Country Party (now the National Party) who was also the Federal Treasurer, Arthur Fadden.

I can still remember a couple of things that were said. Dr Evatt said "The Country Party has no policy, and the Liberal Party, poor little". Mr Fadden complained that Dr Evatt's earlier speech had sounded like a quiz show (such as Bob Dyer's *Pick-a-Box*) where all sorts of prizes were being promised. Politics doesn't change greatly, except that politicians seem to have become more boring, in the main. Or am I just nostalgic?

As an aside, years later in 1975 I sat next to a fellow teacher who was a rusted-on Labor supporter and had at one time been the local campaign secretary for Dr Evatt in his electoral division of Barton. On the morning of 12th November, the day after the Governor-General, Sir John Kerr, had relieved Gough Whitlam of the burden of office as Prime Minister, I approached Peg with trepidation, expecting her to be very upset by what had happened. When

I said "What do you think of Kerr's action?" she replied "What else could he do?" I could go on- and on- and on- about Mr Whitlam's dismissal, but I won't. Well, not on and on- just on.

When Gough Whitlam and the Labor Party won the 1972 federal election it was the first time Labor had been in power since 1949, almost exactly twenty-three years. It was a long time to be out of power and all the ministers from the previous Labor government had left Parliament. There were in fact very few members in the parliament, in either the Senate or the House of Representatives, who had been there when Labor was last in power.

One of Mr Whitlam's problems was that he had a ministry of men- no women- who had no actual experience of government, at least federally. The problem was made worse for him because the Party wanted all ministers to be in Cabinet, causing the body to be somewhat unwieldy. The new government began to do things very quickly and many people in the nation thought he was being too radical too soon as well as being rash in some of his decisions and actions.

In 1973, about a year and a half after Labor came to power, the Opposition in the Senate threatened to deny Supply to the government, thus making it impossible for the government to get the money it needed to govern. So the Prime Minister immediately went to the Governor-General and advised him to call an election. Both Houses of Parliament were dissolved and an election was held for the House of Representatives and the whole of the Senate instead of the usual half-Senate election every three years. Labor won with a reduced majority in the House.

In October 1975 the Opposition again refused to vote either for or against Supply, but this time Mr Whitlam refused to budge. For several weeks there was speculation about what would happen if the Opposition continued its stance, which it did. Would the Governor-General act and if he did, how?

Would he dare to dismiss the government and force an election? In the end, on the last possible day to call an election before the end of the year, the Governor-General, Sir John Kerr, dismissed the government and swore in Malcolm Fraser as Prime Minister.

He did so on the condition that Mr Fraser would advise him to call an election and that no decisions would be made by the new government until after the election. There was much debate on whether Sir John Kerr acted rightly. My own view is the two "villains" in the piece were Mr Whitlam and Mr Fraser. In my opinion the Opposition should not have delayed Supply, but once they did Mr Whitlam should have asked for an election, as he had done the previous year.

It seems that Sir John Kerr acted without warning Gough Whitlam because he feared that the Prime Minister might advise the Queen to dismiss him and appoint a different Governor-General. One aspect of the Australian Constitution is that in these matters of dealing with ministers and a parliament that won't grant supply, the Governor-General has all the power and the Monarch (the King or Queen) has none. He felt obliged to tell the Queen of his actions straight after he had carried them out. In the model of a republic that was put to the voters and rejected in 1999 the President would have much the same powers as the Governor-General has, but the Prime Minister and the President would both have the power to sack the other one.

Looking back now it is probably a good thing that model was not accepted by the people. If we do become a republic (and we may have become one by the time you read this) it is to be hoped that the model presented to the people is less precarious than that. Just for the record, I think the system we have at present (in 2025) works well and does not need to be changed. It took centuries to develop and it could be hazardous to try a new system. But nothing on this earth lasts forever! There is more about Prime Minsters later.

Sitting in the Gallery

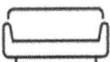

One thing I have liked to do since the 1960s is to sit in the gallery of a house of parliament. I have done so in Canberra, Sydney, Brisbane, Hobart and Perth. In the old Parliament House in Canberra back in the 1960s a member of the public could walk up the stairs, into King's Hall and into one of the house galleries without seeing or experiencing any obvious security personnel or measures. In King's Hall a visitor would sometimes find himself or herself walking close to the Prime Minister and other parliamentarians. Not so in the current building.

There was one junior-looking uniformed policemen in the gallery and presumably a plain-clothed detective or other security person or two lurking somewhere. These days there is a strict security check before admission to the current building and a second, even stricter check before admission to a gallery. Anna and I had the interesting experience in 1972 of sitting in the Speaker's Gallery of the old building while the House was in session where we were seated just behind the members, some of whom had to push past us to get to their seats. It was fun seeing characters such as Gough Whitlam, Fred Daly and Jim Killen at close quarters and in action. On another occasion, in 1975, I was sitting behind a new member called John Howard and was impressed by his ability to speak without notes. On that occasion I achieved my ambition of being locked in the House while a vote was in progress.

A change in attitudes and practices regarding security at Parliament House can be illustrated by an incident that happened in 1975. I was walking around the old building and as I walked a car drew up near me. The Prime Minister, Gough Whitlam, stepped out of the car a few metres in front of me and walked into the building through a side door. The only other people in sight were the car driver moving off and a lone cyclist going past. The new Parliament House provides much more security in a number of ways but there was a more friendly atmosphere with the old one.

> Hansard is the name given to the written record of parliamentary speeches and in fact anything that is said by a member of either a lower or an upper house in State and Federal Parliaments. The words are recorded by a Hansard reporter as they are spoken and can be corrected or altered to some extent before the printed record becomes permanent. If a listener repeats something he or she has heard in a parliament there are two reasons why quoting what was heard may be inaccurate. The listener's memory may not be perfect or the speaker may have altered it after reading the first printed proof of the day. It's also possible that the Hansard reporter made a mistake. Until about the 1970s most reporters took down what was said in shorthand with pen or pencil and paper. Since then typing machines have been increasingly used. An audio recording is also made to assist checking.
>
> The reporter has to be alert for "interjections" by members. Anything that is answered or acknowledged by a current

speaker has to be part of the record. I remember back in the 1960s an incident I didn't hear, but I did tune in to the radio shortly afterwards as the matter was being debated. The Liberal Prime Minister, John Gorton, had been speaking and a seasoned journalist named Alan Ramsey called out from the Press Gallery "You liar!". That began a debate about what to do with Mr Ramsey. A former Leader of the Opposition was adamant that he should be brought before the Bar of the House, sentenced and punished. In the end he got away with it. My most interesting memory of the day is that Hansard clearly had a problem because only Member's words were normally recorded. They solved the problem by characterising Mr Ramsey as "A Voice".

Writing letters

These two paragraphs foreshadow a coverage of letters written to newspapers and other journals, but it might be mentioned that I had lots of letter-writing practice during the year that Anna and I were "courting" and preparing for marriage. We met at a Teachers' Christian Fellowship conference in Canberra just under a year before we married and for nearly all that time I was in Sydney and Anna was in Brisbane. We wrote a voluminous number of letters to one another and for some months I wrote one almost every day, as did Anna. In those day of course there was no email. Nor were there mobile phones. Long-distance phone calls, "trunk" calls, were expensive and we used them rarely. That made good old-fashioned letter-writing our communication method of choice. But back to the current topic.

Writing letters to newspapers and magazines has been one of my delights over the years. I think my first published letter was to a student paper in the mid-1960s and my first letter published in a major newspaper appeared in the Sydney Morning Herald in about 1966. Although it has been my practice to keep an original copy from publications in my files I don't have one of that particular letter. From memory, it had something to do with my perceived "dumbing-down" of university courses. Also in the 1960s I wrote the first letter published in the Sydney Anglican magazine *Southern Cross*, a magazine still going today. More details are given later as the narrative continues, with plenty of examples to enthral or bore the reader (that's you!)

Education

My education included two years at Alexander Mackie (teachers') College followed by a degree painstakingly gained while working as a teacher. Another bit of study earned the Certificate in Theology through Moore Theological College in Sydney and after I retired the study of ancient Greek brought a Graduate Diploma in Humanities, most of the units being in classical Greek. The degree and diploma were both studied through The University of New England in Armidale, a town in northern New South Wales. A Certificate in Arts was added for good measure. No master's degree, no doctorate, no honours- but I have learnt a little along the way. Studying ancient Greek for several years in my sixties was quite a challenge but I had finished gainful employment and had plenty of spare time. It was mostly very enjoyable, in spite of those three-hour examinations. They were quite tiring!

When I was studying part-time for my degree in the 1960s I had to decide what subjects to take. In those days nine units were required for the degree and one that I chose almost accidentally was geography. On completion of a "major" in that subject it seemed natural to change from primary teaching and teach geography in high schools, which I did, among other subjects.

A Job or Two

My first job after my school days was as a clerk in the Commonwealth Conciliation and Arbitration Commission registry. One memory is the frequent appearance of a notice relevant to our office in the Commonwealth Gazette. "Notice of Application for Registration of an Association as an Organisation under the Conciliation and Arbitration Act." The department of which I was an employee (an "officer"!) was that of the Commonwealth Attorney-General. Dealing with the public at the counter and on the telephone was a highlight of the job and I stayed there for two years until I decided that teaching would be a much more interesting and useful career to follow.

At first I took up a position at Barker College in Hornsby, a suburb of Sydney, but when my period of probation was over it had not worked out and I left there to attend teachers' college to be properly trained. That was in 1959 at the time of the Billy Graham meetings in Sydney, an exciting time for evangelical Christians all over Australia as Dr Graham travelled around the nation.

The initial placement when teachers' college days were over was to a little town named Goodooga in north-western New South Wales, a remote town with a mainly Aboriginal population, a hot summer climate and a school with three teachers, soon to grow to four. One thing for which I have always been grateful is that the young headmaster (as male principals were called in former days) was very enthusiastic and genuinely devoted to the students in the school and to the development and welfare of his young teachers. His name was David Maher and he went on years later to a very senior position in the Department of Education. A competition held by the ABC in the 1960s resulted in Goodooga being voted "the most boring town in Australia". An Aboriginal town character known as Shillin' Jackson, when asked were Goodooga was, would draw a circle on the ground and put a dot outside it. "The circle is the world and the dot is Goodooga". (A shilling coin was nominally the same as ten cents)

My first classroom in Goodooga

The academic year at Alexander Mackie College went from September to August. Our 1959 intake was the second group to enter the college and lack of accommodation meant that we were located for most of our first term at what had been Randwick Boys' High School, a place with only basic facilities. My notice of employment at Goodooga, a place I had to find on a map, came near the end of August 1961 with the instruction to report for duty on 12th September, 1961. Some days before I left home for the twenty-four hour journey by a steam mail train, motor train, mixed goods and passenger steam train (*very* slow) followed by a mail truck for the last 120 kilometres, someone on a phone call asked me if "Miss Morrison" was going to the town as a teacher.

The young lady who called and those with her were apparently very pleased when I said "No, Mr Morrison. A male." I hope they liked having me in the town, although they never told me so! The Department of Education in the end appointed a male because it was thought the accommodation was too primitive for a woman. I suppose that policy is known as diversity, equity, inclusion, but let a male take the rap. But I do agree with their reasoning.

Teaching in the local hall

In my experience there are people around who fit the mould of Stephen Leacock's Man in the Pullman Car. He wrote many gently humorous essays on various topics but especially on the foibles of people in various walks of life. A Pullman Car was a type of railway carriage common in the United States in the early twentieth century and the Man mentioned was someone who could talk- and talk and talk- saying along the way many idiosyncratic things. Another type of person I have experienced is The Man who Claps First. He appears at most classical musical concerts and recitals and he is of course usually the one who gives the first (loud) clap just as the music stops, or slightly before. He even sometimes claps when he shouldn't, taking some of the sheep with him. Listen for him next time you attend a concert. But read on- you'll meet some of these characters in more detail later.

But back to the Arbitration Commission. One of the people who used to come into the relatively small office at the Arbitration Commission was a barrister called Lionel Murphy. I didn't get to know him personally then but some years later he appeared in Goodooga as he campaigned for the Labor candidate in the 1963 Federal election. By that time he was Senator Murphy. Another teacher and I had a good talk and argument with him and the next morning he came into my classroom briefly. He later became Leader of the Government in the Senate and Attorney-General in the Whitlam Government. I mention him because he was a very controversial member of the Government.

He was appointed a Justice of the High Court and at one stage was sent to trial and found guilty of perverting the course of justice. At a re-trial he was found not guilty and sadly lived only a short time longer as he was then dying from cancer. Another man I met at the counter of the Commission was a solicitor whom my superiors in the office referred to (behind his back of course) as "Shifty". He was in later years in the news in connection with Lionel Murphy and Neville Wran, a Premier of New South Wales for some years.

Christian Work

My life outside education and work included a definite Christian commitment I made at the age of sixteen. That meant that in the years that followed I was very much involved in Christian work of some kind, including teaching Sunday School, working at beach missions and Christian camps and being involved with the Young People's Fellowship at our church. There were also the Christian groups in high schools. That was no doubt the main commitment I made in life, followed by the momentous decision about seventeen years later when I asked a Christian lady to marry me. More of that later. My main time-consuming Christian work at present (2025) is leading a Bible study group that I have been leading in our house for 27 years.

With regard to residential camps and conferences, and one weekend working bee at Mount Victoria, years ago I jotted down a list of camps and conferences that I had attended and it came to a total of sixty. They included youth fellowship weekends, the Anglican Camp Howard and camps run by Scripture Union, all of which were examples of time away to hear Christian teaching and of course to have a great time together. As mentioned, it was at a combined Inter-Varsity Fellowship and Teachers' Christian Fellowship conference in Canberra in January 1971 that I met Anna, who became my wife one year later. On the few occasions when I organised and ran Scripture Union camps I was called the "commandant", later "changed to "commodore" because it was a sailing camp.

How I was ever supposed to run a sailing camp I will never know, but suffice it to say there wasn't much sailing done apart from fun on a couple of rowing boats and a small boat or two with a small sail. The person immediately below the commandant in command was the "adjutant"- another very military term. I was an adjutant for one camp, thoroughly enjoying keeping the programme running smoothly and keeping the "troops" in order. One adjutant I had when I was commandant was not very good at the job, requiring me to tell him regularly what to do, the wrong way round for the roles. Though a bit eccentric he was good to work with. We ran the camps on quasi-military lines in those days, but those fun days have long since gone. There is in my opinion a strong case for boys-only and girls-only camps, but that idea goes against some modern thinking.

Life in Goodooga

As well as multifarious examples of meetings with human beings in all sorts of places over the years there were also encounters with snakes. On one occasion during my stint as teacher in Goodooga two teaching colleagues and two bank employees joined me in my car for a drive on the dirt road to Brewarrina, about 120 kilometres away (called 76 miles in those days). There we boarded a Fokker Friendship plane for the last three hops of its round trip from Sydney to Charleville in Queensland. The "special" return fare for that journey was three pounds, about one hundred dollars in 2024 terms and cheap for an airfare in those days. On the way home, after leaving the plane at Brewarrina, we stopped near Narran Lake and walked around in the longish grass and reeds.

We were walking in single file and Bill, a teaching colleague, said at one stage "That's dangerous". Then I saw Tom, one of the bank men, jump and utter an exclamation of alarm. I wondered what was going on until I spied a large brown snake beside me, moving very quickly. I assume it was getting out of my way- otherwise I might not be typing this now- but I know that I probably broke both the Olympic high jump and long jump records in one bound.

The really unfortunate thing was that I had put in my pocket a very valuable fountain pen given to me by an uncle- it was a gold Parker 51- and it came out of my pocket into the long grass. As far as I know it is there still. The irony is that I had put it in my pocket to make sure it was with me rather than in the not-very-secure little house we three teachers occupied.

Tales could be told about that house. It was really a garage with a side annex. The walls were simply sheets of "fibro" with no lining of any kind. The roof was galvanised iron, with no ceilings. It was very cold on winter's nights, but it did cool down quickly at night in the very hot summers. One morning I stood on my bed and scraped frost off the underside of the roof. For my first four terms in the town (we had three-term years in those days) we assistant teachers lived in the local hotel. It was reasonably comfortable if a bit primitive (I won't mention the bathroom arrangements) and provided three adequate meals per day.

Things were sometimes rather rowdy at weekends when shearers came in from the sheep station and spent a couple of days relaxing and drinking. When new proprietors took over and eventually reduced the food supply and raised the tariff we sought different accommodation and were able to move into that little fibro and iron hovel we called home. The old Silent Knight kerosene-burner refrigerator kept our food cool, at least in winter. It was largely useless in hot summer weather when we needed it most.

While I was at Goodooga two of us teachers and the policeman's wife conducted a "Sunday school" on Wednesdays afternoons after school. We held it in the combined Presbyterian-Methodist church building. For a while we tried Sunday as the appropriate day but almost no one came. The numbers were never high on either day. We battled on mid-week but that was not connected to the fact that Wednesday is named after Woden, the supposed god of war.

On the Way to Goodooga

My first driving test was in January, 1963 and the next one was in February, 2024. My brother Robert had given me a few driving lessons in the 1950s, but my licence didn't eventuate until the day I took delivery of my new car. My Uncle Clive came with me to pick the car up one morning and I picked up the licence that afternoon. My very first afternoon of driving improved a lot when I finally remembered to drive with the handbrake off.

As a novice driver it was quite an adventure to set off back to Goodooga a few weeks later with a drive of about eight hundred kilometres ahead before arriving back at the hotel where three of us teachers lived at the time. Another teacher and I travelled to Coonamble the first day and stayed overnight at a motel. The first day's travel was very smooth and it was a good opportunity for me to get used to country driving. The other teacher didn't have his licence and thus I alone had to drive.

The next day was a different story. For a while we travelled on a bitumen road but before long the bitumen ended and we were on a gravel or dirt road. What is still vivid in my mind is the fact that there had been heavy rain in recent days and the surface was very wet and muddy. We and several other cars soon found ourselves bogged and as each car moved on a couple of hundred metres and was bogged again, the drivers and passengers walked back to help others move on. We eventually arrived in Walgett and since most of the cars were not going our way- towards Lightning Ridge and Goodooga- we set off in our car alone and hoped to reach Goodooga in time for the evening meal.

˙˙

The distance was about 140 kilometres and was almost all on dirt road, the "dirt" being heavy clay soil. It was a good thing that the soil was very wet and not just "tacky" because in the latter case it would have built up on the wheels and forced us to stop every few hundred metres to perform the tedious and difficult task of cleaning the tyres. With much slipping and sliding we eventually reached Goodooga, after stopping at Lightning Ridge for a while. David Maher, our Headmaster, was amazed to see us arrive in town, having already informed the Inspector in Moree that the Goodooga staff would probably arrive several days late. In the event we were ready to teach the next day, the first day of school for the year. We must have *seemed* excessively keen.

But that's not all! As we were returning to Goodooga later in the year we became bogged in the middle of the road early in the evening and were stuck until after daylight appeared. The other teacher slept for much of the night, but I made sure I was awake the whole night so that I could turn on my lights if I saw another vehicle coming. Very few did, but I remember at least one big truck and a smaller vehicle. Again the Headmaster was surprised to see us back at school almost on time, this time being able to start before lunchtime on the first day of term.

Sydney Morrison Once More

Even though my father's service in the First World War was before my time, unlike his Second World War experience, it is worthy of being related further. He enlisted in the First AIF (Australian Infantry Force) in 1916 and served in France and Belgium in 1917 until he was badly wounded with a concussive blow to the head from an artillery shell. He was wounded at Ypres in Belgium on 4th October, 1917. His rank was Lance Corporal and he had been awarded the Military Medal for "bravery in the field". The convalescent home he was sent to in England was one of many of the kind set up during the war. One interesting and poignant document from that time is a letter he wrote to his oldest sister Cath while he was convalescing in England before returning to Australia. Some of it is reproduced here.

My Dear Sister,

Am once more in Blighty [that is, Britain]*, and it is tres* (sic) *bon, after France. We call it all France, but most of my fighting experiences have been in Belgium, and it is a warm part of the globe, especially Messines and Ypres. I was wounded at the latter place…Happened to get it in the head, but my steel lid saved my life. I got a nasty smack, fracturing my skull, and rendering my left arm useless…The treatment here is all that could be desired, the food excellent, and everybody are* (sic) *anxious to do all they can for us. It is a fine mansion, in the heart of the Epping Forest, and* *is controlled entirely by voluntary aid...Can write with a certain amount of freedom from England, but can't give my opinion of the war, as [General] Haig might not like it, and Haig and I don't always agree...Take care of those photos of my mates as most of them have been killed, and would not like to lose them as they are nice to have.*

The Sister

Sydney's sister Catherine Morrison was born in 1885 and was the oldest of the surviving Morrison children. Another had died at a very young age. Both parents had died by the turn of the century and Cath and her brother James (known by his second name, Arthur) more or less brought up the other three. Cath started her first job in 1899 at Grace Brothers in Sydney (always written as "Grace Bros") and her starting salary was two shillings and sixpence, that being twenty-five cents in decimal currency, worth about twenty-five dollars in 2025 terms. It wasn't even enough to cover her fares to and from work, but before long the firm doubled the amount to five shillings per week. Her hours of work were very long and she finished the week at 9:00 PM on Saturdays. There were no facilities for employees and she had to sit in the park opposite to eat her lunch and use the facilities there. That job finished in 1907 when she had found other employment and the management of Grace Bros gave her an excellent reference with the general comment "We have always found Miss Morrison honest, willing, obliging and attentive to her duties". It would seem to me that she was well and truly exploited by one of the leading firms in Sydney! The original of that reference is at present in my possession. And now. Let's turn to music, that happy place with those with ears to hear.

Music

My musical career, if my playing here and there could be given that grand title, began just before my nineteenth birthday when I began piano lessons with a lady called Leila M. Sparke, a neighbour across the road, in her day a very good pianist. A couple of years later I began organ lessons as well with our church organist, a gentleman name Ken Keck, whose initials incidentally were K. E. C. K. By the time I was sent to Goodooga at the age of twenty-two I had sufficient skill to play hymns for the local churches and to play the piano for school and town events.

Many years later I took organ lessons again for about two years from Robert Ampt, the Sydney City Organist who held that position for well over forty years. Playing for church services has been my main musical activity over the years and I relinquished the role in 2023 at the age of eighty-four. I may have continued longer if it were not for circumstances changing, one of which turned out to be finding a good replacement.

When I lived in Goodooga from September 1961 to December 1963 I was the organist for all Anglican, Presbyterian and Methodist services during school terms. That was no great burden since the Anglican minister came once a fortnight, the Presbyterian man once a month and the two Methodist deaconesses once every two or three months. The many Anglican services were held on Sundays but the other two denominations had mid-week services. The Presbyterian and Methodist services were held in the same building while the Anglicans had their own building. There was also a small Roman Catholic church building in the town and it had regular visits by a priest.

One night I began the first hymn at the Methodist service and as I began, a mosquito bit me on the nose. At that stage my playing was not so secure that I would dare try to hit the mossie. So I simply endured the bite and the itch that followed. Some might say that my playing then was not up to scratch. On another occasion I arrived at the church to practise on the little "American" organ and found that its innards had been gnawed by rats and it was almost unplayable. The Methodist deaconesses from Brewarrina found a replacement instrument at Girilambone (not to be confused with Gulargambone). The organs were not harmoniums. The "American" organ works on suction while a harmonium blows the air over the reeds. Suction gives a louder and clearer sound. It is much more satisfying of course to play a pipe organ or a large modern electronic organ with full pedalboard.

The organ in the Sydney Town Hall. I have enjoyed playing it for my own amusement.

Thoughts (mine)

Some of my thoughts on being a church organist may be of interest to the reader, especially if this is being read posthumously (concerning me, not the reader!):

Letter to *The Sydney Organ Journal*   About 2003

Morwena Campbell-Smith's "Beginner's Guide to Playing at Funerals" in the winter Journal gives good advice to new organists and brings a smile to the face of one who is in his latter days of organ playing (and is no doubt in his latter days-full stop!). The late arrival or non-arrival of the printed form of service for both weddings and funerals is a well-known phenomenon. Some years ago I was playing at a friend's funeral and the form arrived well before the service began but had one of the hymns missing. We had to make the quick decision to hand out hymn books after all. And so it goes on, with most seasoned organists having a multitude of stories to tell. Some of us have had the unnerving experience of realising that the congregation has forms of service which the organist has not seen. These days I play only at funerals where the deceased or the family has specially asked me to do so, one advantage being that there are usually plenty of churchgoers present and they know the hymns; and they actually sing!

The advice that made me smile most when reading the article was the reference to obituaries lasting "for these brief minutes". "And the rest", I thought. At one funeral I played at this year the obituaries went for more than an hour and the service went for two hours. I understand that is not unusual. Another funeral which, mercifully, I watched on live-stream because of the crowds expected (no organ required), had obituaries lasting two hours. The deceased man had been involved in many things and was larger than life, but expecting people to sit through a service lasting well over two hours is somewhat thoughtless. If anyone has anything to say about me at my funeral, I hope the total "eulogy" time does not exceed twenty minutes, the rest of the time focussing on Christ and what he has done and is doing. Incidentally, the service leader (to use the modern phrase) might take the opportunity to inform those present that organists use both feet, heel and toe. It's amazing what some seasoned churchgoers don't know.

One fellow-organist at Christ Church Springwood was a man called Fred Birkett. He was tragically killed in 2004 and Robert Ampt, at the time President of the Organ Music Society of Sydney, asked me to write an article about Fred for the *Sydney Organ Journal*. Some of it is inserted here in the spirit of this book as partly an account of the world around me. I have edited out some whole paragraphs for reasons of space

An Unforgettable Character

At one time Readers' Digest had a regular feature called "The Most Unforgettable Character I've Met". Fred Birkett was an unforgettable character to those who knew him. Elsewhere in this issue his Obituary outlines his musical career. I have been asked to make some observations and reflections on Fred the man as I and others saw him.

When a fellow organist of Christ Church, Springwood, rang me on the morning of Friday, March 19, it was disturbing to hear that Fred Birkett had had a serious accident and would be out of action for some time. It was much more disturbing a little later to learn that his injuries were such that he probably would not recover. During a lunch break on a drive to Canberra I learnt the sad news that Fred had indeed succumbed to his injuries. As is usual in such circumstances, shock and disbelief remained for days amongst those who knew him.

Fred lived in Springwood for about fifteen years and for about the last ten he was part-time organist at two Anglican churches, St Marks, Granville and Christ Church, Springwood. At Springwood he was, with me and two others, on the organ roster for the only weekly parish service where the organ is regularly used. If things had happened in chronological order I would have gone first and Fred would have been third, but life is rarely like that.

Fred was also a man of very decided opinions and was not reluctant in bringing them to the fore. Some years ago I spent a few hours trying many of the 200 main settings available on our church electronic organ and finally settled on one that seemed right for the building. It was a warmer sound than the previous one and had a slight reverberation. The other two organists were very happy with the sound but Fred was most displeased. I then spent more time looking for a switch and working out how to link it up so that the reverberation could be switched off. Since then I have called it the "Fred switch". Fred's ideas on organ sounds were definitely further from the romantic than ours, and I don't think he liked reeds very much. Although we often differed in our opinions, there was never any doubt that Fred was a man with knowledge, skill, and dedication. My remaining fellow organists will not mind if I say that he was clearly the most skilled organist among us four.

It must be said that Fred was decidedly not one of those to whom Alexander Pope referred when he wrote of people "who to the church repair, not for the doctrine but the music there". If he thought the minister had taught some dubious doctrine he showed no reluctance in telling him so and giving him his reasons.

Anyone who met Fred in the street (especially in Springwood on Saturday mornings) had to be ready for a brisk discussion on any of a range of topics. His knowledge of early church history (including the biblical accounts) was made more real to him by his travels in Mediterranean lands. To be with him as he showed his photos and discussed the significance of the places he visited was an interesting and informative experience. He liked to travel when time and money permitted and had made final bookings for a trip to the outback just before his death.

Writing letters to newspapers was another of Fred's occupations in recent years. His views were of course stated strongly. The letters were always interesting and usually provocative. Recently he had one published in The Blue Mountains Gazette, defending Christian belief. Typically of Fred he was able to get in the last word as it were by having a letter appearing posthumously in Southern Cross, the Sydney Anglican newspaper. Some people eye with suspicion those who write regularly to newspapers, while others of us see it as a very important activity in general community debate. We know that Fred was never one to shrink from debate, public or private. At his funeral we learnt of his propensity for vigorous discussion at lunchtime at his place of work. That was no surprise.

Christ Church at Springwood was full for the funeral on Thursday, March 25. The presence of some of Sydney's leading organists was a tribute to his years of loyal service in and through music. Fred had chosen his funeral hymns about 30 years earlier (he was a man who believed in careful planning!). The strife is o'er, the battle won and For all the saints, who from their labours rest. One was a song of triumph about his risen Lord and the other reminded us of the eternal destiny of those who acknowledge Jesus as Saviour and Lord. There was shock and sadness at both Fred's passing and the manner of it, but there was joy in knowing that he is now safe from the perils and dangers of this life. He was truly an unforgettable character. I'm glad I knew him.

David Morrison   April 2, 2004

No traveller

I have been a stay-in-Australia sort of person for most of my life. Life in the slow lane, you might say. The only other countries I have visited are New Zealand, Vanuatu, New Caledonia and Fiji. My first trip outside of New South Wales was a train trip to Canberra in 1942 at the age of three. I didn't go outside that state again until I crossed the border in 1962 to play the organ at a wedding while living in Goodooga. In fact two weddings in Queensland were the total of interstate weddings for which I was the organist. The rest were in New South Wales, and there were plenty of those. Compared to the travels of many today my adventures are hardly worth a mention. One interesting memory of the wedding in Hebel in Queensland is the minister announcing a hymn and then disappearing into the vestry with the bridal party. I played an introduction and then all the verses of the hymn But I couldn't hear anyone singing. One guest assured me later that he was singing. I believed his evidence.

> Sir Robert Menzies in Parliament:
> W C Wentworth, the (Liberal) Member for Mackellar: Has shortage of business in the House occurred as part of a deliberate Cabinet plan in contempt of Parliament, or because of Cabinet's incapacity to prepare its business properly and promptly for submission to Parliament; or for some other cause?
>
> Menzies: For some other cause.

Christian Thinking

My understanding of Christian matters has been greatly enhanced by two streams of experience which occurred mainly during our marriage. One was the completion of the Certificate of Theology through Moore Theology College in Sydney. The other was the reading of works by and about great Christian leaders, mainly from the time of the Protestant Reformation to the present. The Moore College course was invaluable in clarifying my thoughts as I learnt more and more about the Bible and related subjects. My general Christian reading broadened that experience and gave me some increased awareness of and knowledge of the great subject matter of Theology- God. Great Christians who were the subject of my reading include sixteenth century Reformers such as Martin Luther, John Calvin and several others. Later men included the Puritans such as John Owen and John Bunyan in the seventeenth century, George Whitfield and John and Charles Wesley in the eighteenth, Bishop J C Ryle and C H Spurgeon in the nineteenth and Martyn Lloyd-Jones in the twentieth. The complete list of course is much longer.

C S Lewis wrote that one thing that bothered him when he was an atheist was that books written by Christians, on whatever subject, always seemed to be more interesting than books written by unbelievers. He became a great apologist (one who argues in favour of something) for the Christian faith. I have read several books by Lewis and have always found him very readable, including his monumental book on English literature of the sixteenth century. Some parts of that book are hard going, but clever Lewis-ish comments and observations appear at regular intervals. It's worth reading if you don't mind a bit of mental effort. He of course had a great intellect but could express things in simple and homely terms when appropriate.

Marriage

Earlier I mentioned that the second biggest commitment I made in my life was to marry the lady who became the mother of our five children. We had both gone to Canberra in January, 1971, to attend a conference put on by the Teacher's Christian Fellowship, the conference being held concurrently with that of the Inter-Varsity Fellowship, better known these days as the Australian Fellowship of Evangelical students. The morning talks were given by the Reverend Dr John Stott, a well-known preacher and teacher from London. Those of us at the teacher's conference joined the IVF people for Dr Stott's talk before morning tea and then went back for our own programme for the rest of the day. On about the first or second day I spied a lady sitting almost opposite, just along the meal table from me and, as the saying goes, the rest is history. Anna returned to Brisbane with her brother Paul a day early and I decided to write a letter to her at her Brisbane address. I'm not sure how I found the address, but I think it was listed in some conference information. Thanks for that, conference organiser!

I gather that Anna was not particularly surprised to receive the letter and a reply from her arrived very soon afterwards. When I walked through the front door on arriving home I had said to my mother "Guess what?" She threw up at least one hand and said, almost in dismay, "You've met a girl!". My sister had been married about ten days earlier and I think Mum (I called her Mum but she was my mother, not my "mum"!) was hoping that she would have me at home for a bit longer before the inevitable meeting of a woman who would become my wife. But I was nearly thirty-two! Time was running out and I had met The One.

Needless to say that, as mentioned earlier, in those pre-email and expensive telephone call days we both became prolific at letter-writing, Anna in her beautiful handwriting and I in my... and we got to the stage of writing almost every day. There were trips to and from Brisbane and we were married on New Year's Day, 1972, by the Reverend Mr Westera in the Reformed Church at Toowong, an inner suburb of Brisbane. That weatherboard church building has long since gone to make way for home units or villas or whatever the appropriate word is. We have never had trouble remembering the date of our wedding anniversaries! Often we "see our anniversary in" as we also see in the New Year, and even a new Millennium on 1st January, 2001. After a honeymoon at Binna Burra in the Lamington National Park, just north of the New South Wales-Queensland border, we came to Springwood. Until July we lived in a home unit near the highway and then moved into our newly-built house, where at the time of writing we have lived since.

Springwood

When we arrived in Springwood the township seemed a mixture of a Sydney suburb and a country town. If I remember correctly the Bureau of Statistics had Springwood outside the official area of Sydney at the time, but not long afterwards Sydney was said to stretch as far west as Faulconbridge. "Greater Sydney" now includes all the townships in the Blue Mountains. There is still a feeling for many of us that we are still outside Sydney, with the surrounding bushland (mostly dry sclerophyll forest) helping that non-urban sense to persist.

The "bush" is of course subject to fires from time to time and we remember especially the fires of 1978, 1994, 2001 and 2013. The very hot early summer of 2019-2020 also had severe fires in the mountains but rain in January came before the fires were able to threaten us. From that point onwards we had relatively cool summers for a few years and of course the very heavy rains of early 2020 came just before the COVID pandemic changed our lives dramatically for a while.

Springwood was named by Governor Macquarie in 1815 when he noticed a stream flowing through a "wood", another name for an area of forest or bushland. That of course was a little earlier than my time!

A Vegetarian's Lament

In the 1940s there was a mention in the in the Sydney Morning Herald of the playwright George Bernard Shaw and his vegetarian habits. Someone alleged that he had eaten large amounts of beef extract over many years. My aunt, Catherine Morrison, wrote to him and asked if it were true. He put her address on an envelope and replied by writing across her letter, in red ink, "It's a flat lie. I haven't tasted beef for forty years. GBS". The red ink seems appropriate because Shaw was politically towards the red end of the political spectrum (a spectrum which has become very confused in recent times). At the time of writing the envelope and letter are in my possession. The full text of Catherine's letter is:

Dear Sir,

In the SYDNEY MORNING HERALD dated 28th March 1947 the following paragraph appears in Column 8-H. *Kefford- general secretary of the Meat and Allied Trades' Federation-told the Millions Club yesterday that Bernard Shaw, as the foremost vegetarian, was a fraud.* "He's been taking beef extract under doctor's orders for years", he said. *An American doctor calculated that Shaw*

> *consumed beef extract the equivalent of 257,687 pounds of steak a year.*
>
> The above calculation seems to be worked out very finely. Will you please advise me if the statement which appeared in THE SYDNEY MORNING HERALD is correct. If not, it should be refuted.

The letter was signed off in the usual polite way:

> With kind regards and awaiting your reply.
>
> Yours faithfully,
> (Miss C A Morrison)

When I first knew her and until her very late years Auntie Cath was largely a vegetarian. All three aunties were advised by Doctor Pedersen in later years to eat some red meat, presumably mainly to ensure a sufficient intake of iron.

Those aunties, my father's three sisters, lived next door to us. They never married and the only progeny from the family were my father's three children and his brother's son, Bruce. His brother Arthur and wife Margaret did adopt a girl in the 1940s but sadly she died at about four years of age. The three sisters from eldest to youngest were Catherine Alice (Auntie Cath), Emilia Rose Clair (Auntie Millie) and Flora Isabella (Auntie Flora). Flora lived to ninety-nine but the other two fell far short of that. The family of five were left to look after themselves when their parents died by the turn of the century and they did a marvellous job of it, especially Cath and Arthur as they looked after the younger ones who were about eight and ten years old at the time.

As mentioned earlier, Cath worked very hard in her first job with Grace Bros (short for Brothers!) in 1898 for two shillings and sixpence per week (twenty-five cents) to her main life's work when she learned to be a an accountant with no formal qualifications. Uncle Arthur ended his career as Collector of Customs in Sydney, head of the customs office in that city. Auntie Flora spent her life as a nurse, including work in outback NSW and in India. Auntie Millie began nursing training but mostly was the housekeeper for the three of them. Flora lived for twenty-eight years after the other two had both died. Sydney spent most of his working life as a floor covering shop assistant at Morley Johnson's small department store near Town Hall railway station in Sydney.

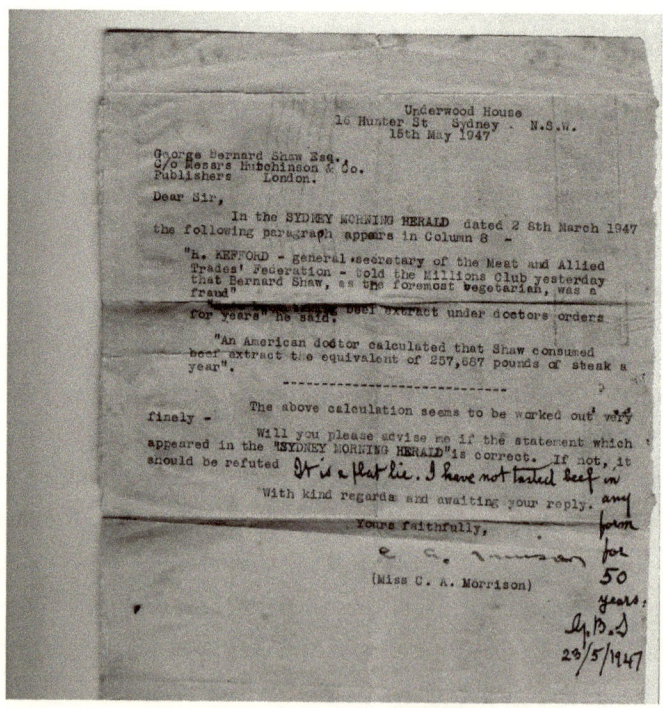

George Bernard Shaw's answer written on Auntie Cath's letter

Teaching Geography

Once I had started teaching for the New South Wales Department of Education I resumed the degree I had started after I left school while I was working for the Commonwealth Government. Once I began it again the going was a bit slow and then speeded up for the second half of the degree requirements. In those days an Arts degree at Sydney and New England Universities involved nine units of work which had to include at least two third year units. At one stage I found it hard to decide which first year subject to study and almost half-heartedly I chose Geography I.

The subject proved to be very interesting and I made the decision to go on to Geography II and III. The third year examination consisted of five three-hour papers and when I had finished I felt that I had expounded quite a bit of the subject. Eventually my enjoyment of geography propelled me to move to a high school position so that I could teach it at higher levels.

I left St Ives North Public School at the end of the first week of Term I in 1971 (a few weeks after I had met Anna!) and the next morning reported for duty at Windsor High School. In those days the change from primary to secondary teaching involved turning up at the high school and being put straight into the classroom, sink or swim. I had the benefit of the first period off and then I was standing at first in front of a Year 7 class ("First Form" in those days) teaching Social Studies, the age group at least being close to what I was used to. After six years at Windsor I was transferred to Springwood High where I taught for ten years, followed by ten years at Winmalee High, followed by retirement.

One very important aspect of teaching is the occasional trip out of the school grounds for what were often called "excursions" but for which we preferred the more grandiose and realistic title "fieldwork". On one occasion I took a bus load of Year Twelve Students to Bathurst for the day so that we could do some fieldwork on urban geography. At one stage I sent them off in groups in different directions and since it was nearly lunchtime I bought a sandwich and began to eat it as I waited for the groups to come back and obtain further instructions. When one group returned I put my partly-eaten sandwich on a seat (on its wrapping of course) and sat on another seat to check in with the students.

As the students walked off I noticed a thin-looking man walk by and eye my sandwich. It seemed mean not to let him pick it up and eat it. He went over, picked it up and off he went. A few seconds later he fulfilled his civic duty and threw it into a bin.

It was always my contention (half seriously) that a teacher of geography was always on duty when out and about. Even lazily looking out of a train window in daytime (other than in tunnels) should cause the geographer to ask himself or herself questions about the landscape(s) visible as the train speeds (or crawls) along. So long as there is some sort of outside view there will be a human or natural landscape, or very often of course a combination of both.

I gave my students three simple questions to think about whenever they were observing a feature of a landscape- What is it? Where is it? Why is it there? A fourth task might be to consider the interactions between that feature and other aspects of the area. Some of my students were not particularly keen to follow my suggestion that next time they were at the beach they should make sure they studied the sand dunes and thought about swash and backwash and longshore drift before plunging into the water. Each to his own, as they say.

Another Snake Story- at the Picture Show

One night at Goodooga in the early 1960s I was seated in the open-air cinema when a cry went up: "There's a snake here!". Most of the snakes we saw there were brown snakes and a big one had enough venom to do a person in comprehensively. The movie stopped and the lights came up and we all stood on our seats, not an easy task since they were canvas seats strung between metal rungs. We all hoped someone would deal with the snake before it dealt with us. From memory, someone killed it and we continued to watch the movie with perhaps not quite so much equanimity as before.

While on the subject of the cinema it might be the time to report on the times the film projector jammed. The film frame that happened to be behind the lens also happened to be in front of the very bright and very hot light bulb. As we watched the still image on the big screen it would develop a small burn mark and then the whole frame would rapidly burn. There would then be a pause while the film was repaired and the projector somehow was started again.

In those days cinema sessions often had a cartoon or two and a "newsreel" or two, short accounts of some items of recent news from Australia and overseas. In city and suburban cinemas the newsreels usually had news from the past week or two, but by the time they reached Goodooga the news was six months to a year old. In the cities at that time there were newsreel theatrettes where about an hour's worth of film was repeated over and over throughout the day. People would go in at any time during the day and leave when the screen showed the newsreel during which they had come in. In an open air cinema of course films could be shown only after dark, and preferably when it wasn't raining. It didn't rain very often in Goodooga. In city cinemas at that time we used to stand for "God Save the King" as the tune was played and images of flags and the monarch came on to the screen as soon as the lights were dimmed for the first film.

Dry Cleaning

Dry cleaning may not seem to be a very interesting topic but one instance sticks in my memory. While living in Goodooga I would hand some clothes for dry cleaning to a shop owner and he would send them by mail truck to Brewarrina where there was a dry cleaning business. On Saturday morning I went into the shop and asked if my dry cleaning had come back and was told "He's bogged at the thirty-nine mile". In other words, the large truck that brought the mail and all sorts of other things to the town was delayed until the driver could somehow extricate the truck from the wet heavy grey soil road.

When I first went to Goodooga I rode in that truck from Brewarrina to Goodooga as it was the only regular public transport from the railway terminus and was only available if a seat in the cabin was available. I don't know the first name of the mail truck driver, but his surname was Webb and he was called "Webby".

Change and Mud

Talking of Goodooga, we had a reunion of teachers in 2010, arranged by David Maher, the Principal from the early 1960s. Three of the four photographs below are from the early 1960s and one is from 2010. The difference in the look of the school was quite remarkable. There was air-conditioning, there were inside toilets, there was a large indoors assembly area and a large covered outdoor area. The school's enrolment was about twenty-five per cent smaller than when we taught there but its staff consisted of about three times the number, including non-teaching staff.

The weekly (sometimes twice-weekly) DC3 from Sydney

The town on the other hand seemed to have gone backwards. The bowling green at the bowling club consisted of weeds and many of the trees in the town had vanished. The hotel had burned down and was replaced by a small tavern. One thing that causes towns to decline is the arrival of all-weather roads from larger centres. People then tend to go to the larger centres more often for shopping, medical appointments and other matters. The roads in my day were all simply dirt with no gravel. The soil was mostly a grey soil (often called "black soil") which had a very high clay content. When the road was wet but not too wet the soil would cling to tyres and build up on the tyres. Sometimes the only solution was to stop every few hundred metres and scrape off the mud and then keep going. The problem was that as the wheel in effect became bigger as the mud built up it would soon refuse to turn as it was stuck in the wheel recess. The road was quite often impassable for all but large trucks, and sometimes even for them. In the same way aeroplanes were unable to land at times.

I remember once driving from Goodooga to Walgett, a distance of about 140 kilometres, on a dry day with plenty of dust being thrown up by my vehicles and others. Some kilometres ahead I saw a small rainstorm move across the road and then disappear, leaving a fine day once more in its train. When I arrived at the place where the rain had fallen on the road I was suddenly confronted with wet road with no warning- at least I had ignored the warning. I found myself out of control and all I could do was sit and wait for the car to slow down and stop with the mud acting as a brake. The car stopped less than a metre from a large white roadside post, with no damage other than a slightly shaken driver. But such incidents are par for the course in that sort of country and are soon put behind one (or in one's epitaph).

Kindergarten, First Class and Second Class (Year 1 and Year 2)

The town centre of Goodooga. Left- The hotel where we lived for some time.

The Local Baker

There was a baker near the Telegraph hotel in Goodooga, located between the hotel and Gunn's Store. He baked bread daily and supplied the hotel and anyone else who wanted to buy it. It was not very well baked and when we had our own abode we regularly bought sliced bread (a relatively new invention then) that came from Walgett a couple of times a week. Gunn's Store was by then not run by the Gunn family but Mr and Mrs Gunn were prominent people in the town. Some called Mr Gunn "Mayor of Goodooga" but that was an unofficial title invested on him by the locals. I met the baker in Sydney a few years later and by then he had moved away with new employment.

Goodooga Public School Staff in 1962
Alan Starrett, David Maher, Ross Walkley and David Morrison

The same staff, in the same positions, very close to the original spot, in 2010

Church Music Once More

The following letter sets out some of my thoughts on church music. In 2024 we moved to a different church service in a different part of the parish, away from the old and beautiful church building where we worshiped for about thirty-seven years. We now have little prayer book use and the music is so-called "contemporary". Although much of the music would not be or first choice we believed that it was time to attend a service with a wider age group rather than sticking with our fellows of relatively advanced age (in our case 81 and 86 at the time of writing- and counting).

The letter was to *The Sydney Organ Journal*, the journal of the Organ Music Society of Sydney in 2008. The word "music" was added to the name of the society when people wondering about organ donations (parts of the human body) were mistaking the Society's *raison d'etre*.

    Dear Sir,

    In the Autumn edition of *The Journal* some comments were made about St Andrews Cathedral in Sydney and about the future of church music there and elsewhere. While agreeing with some of the concerns people have on the subject I find myself a bit ambivalent at times. Like anyone else, we organists can (perhaps unconsciously at times) see ourselves and our craft as the most important thing before and after sliced bread. It is hard to imagine that a Christian with any sort of voice would not want to sing, but beyond that musical instruments, choirs, bands and song-leaders are optional extras (and the last two mentioned are not among my options!).

If we start with St Andrews, it is important to separate fact from myth. In 2004 I was told by a very musical person in a town far from Sydney that the choir had been abolished. On Easter Day this year I went to a Sunday service at St Andrews for the first time in about three years and I observed that a choir which was supposedly dead was taking a long time to lie down. The media has been largely responsible for misrepresentation and distortion, and silly comments about the movable communion table and its new position during communion services were not helpful in taking criticism seriously. Many changes have taken place in Anglican churches in recent decades, including the position of the communion table and where the priest stands, but it seems that Sydney is the only diocese where change is to be forbidden.

The point at issue of course is the use of music in churches, whether in cathedrals or elsewhere. Sometimes we can deprive congregations of the joy of singing when the choir does all the singing except for the hymns. I have been to cathedral services and found it quite frustrating not to be able to join in with the Psalm, the Venite or the Te Deum (and of course Sunday Morning Prayer services with the canticles are hard to find anywhere these days). Even the regulars were unable to join in. Some years ago I attended a midweek Evensong at St Andrews and there was one congregational hymn, with well-known words but sung to a strange tune. A couple of years ago I went to a midweek Evensong at a cathedral in another State capital and there was no congregational participation at all (but since there were only two or three of us it may have been just as well).

There is a view that a choir is singing to God, and therefore it doesn't matter if there is anyone there to hear them, and if there are people present it doesn't really matter whether they are edified or not. I think God wants to hear the praises of *all* his people in word and song, and I doubt whether he is very concerned about consecutive fifths and croaky voices so long as the heart is right and people are not being deliberately slipshod. I am all in favour of fine music in church but, if it is not helping the congregation, efforts should be made to help people appreciate it, and as much as possible of the singing should include the congregation. People really can learn to chant Psalms, sing the Merbecke communion setting (if church tastes warrant it) and join in with some simpler choir settings of the canticles. If a Stanford Te Deum is to be sung, there could be a simple setting of the Venite before it so that everyone can make a joyful noise.

Finally there is the question of the future of organ music. There is no magic formula to make people's tastes conform to ours, and that's a pity, and there's no easy way to stop some clergy from wanting a band, and organs banned. Some organists could learn to be a bit more dramatic in their accompaniments and not be thought of as "stuffy". I am always disappointed for example in "Abide with me" when "shine through the gloom" in the last verse doesn't involve a loud solo stop and the next bit "Heaven's morning breaks" doesn't bring the roof down. One part of the solution of course is for members of the congregation who like organs and traditional music to speak up when changes are being forced through by clergy or pushy lay people. Some clergy don't know much about organs of course. Such a one stood behind me once almost open-mouthed as he watched me a play a pedal solo as though he was observing a miracle. It was of course a miracle that I got the notes right, but he had apparently never noticed before what organists do with the pedals.

Perhaps in the end we have to become more in line with the times in advertising our instrument and its music. We could think of global warming and the need to be green and natural. We could have posters saying " Come to the recital in the Town Hall at lunch time today. Hear beautiful music, the only music that is truly organic". 2008

Spoonerisms

William Archibald Spooner was an English clergyman who lived in England from 1844 to 1930. He was also an Oxford "Don", a term referring to men and women who teach at Oxford University. He was well known for transposing the first letters of words with the first letters of other words. Whether it is true or not I like the story of his reprimanding and "sending down" a lazy and troublesome student. As he faced the student he is supposed to have said "My first objection to your conduct is that you hissed all my mystery lectures. I saw you fight a liar in the courtyard and in fact you have tasted the whole worm. Tonight I am going to send you down from Oxford in the town drain".

On another occasion Dr Spooner was supposedly at a university dinner and he was seated next to the faculty Dean, as senior figure in a university. It was always the practice until recent decades for someone proposing the toast at a formal occasion to propose a toast to the King or Queen first. Queen Victoria was on the throne at the time (which puts the story in the nineteenth century). The Queen was quite old at the time and greatly beloved by her people. Dr Spooner began the toasts by saying "Gentlemen, would you please stand as I propose a toast to the queer old Dean".

LIFE IN THE SLOW LANE

Talking of deans- in about 2007 the Professor of Classics and Ancient History, Greg Horsely, was quite keen on my request to be enrolled in a pass master's degree in classical Greek. The Dean of the faculty thought differently and said he didn't think they should have pass master's degrees in ancient languages, unlike modern languages. I was disappointed, but it saved me a lot of work!

Tiddles and...

While my grandmother and her unmarried daughter Muriel were living with us from the late 1940s to 1955 she liked to call me "Tiddles". I didn't mind the name being used in the privacy of our home but I was mortified one day when she greeted me at the door of the bus and some of my school mates heard her say in a loud voice "Hello Tiddles!"

...the bag

When I worked at the Arbitration Commission we had two locked mail bags that went between our Sydney office and head office in Melbourne. They were used to transfer documents overnight between the two offices, including some documents of a sensitive nature. An employee would take the bag down to the GPO (General Post Office) late in the day and collect the other one first thing in the morning. The Melbourne address, by the way, was in Little Bourke Street. We simply called the bag the "IR", standing for "Industrial Registrar", the title of the boss in Melbourne. One day a man from the post office came to the counter of our Sydney office and told me that we needed to make the address on the label more clear. The previous night the bag had gone to Bourke, a small remote town in New South Wales. I quickly took steps to remedy that!

You may have heard the term "the back o' Bourke". That's the place! On my first trip to Goodooga, by train and mail truck, my second of three trains was the motor train from Nyngan to Bourke, but I had to get off (sorry, alight) at Byrock and wait for a mixed goods and passenger train to Brewarrina. But that is covered elsewhere in this seemingly rambling story. Well, not seemingly. Just rambling.

Prime Ministers

Since my interest in politics blossomed at about the age of twelve I have had an interest in our Prime Ministers, especially the ones I was aware of from Chifley onwards. Some others who were in office after I was born have become an interest in retrospect. The ones before my time fall outside the scope of this book (which saves me from searching for facts about them!) An aspect of their times in office is the various ways they first came to power and the ways they left.

Of those Prime Ministers who were in office in my lifetime, at the time of writing, eight came to power as Leaders of the Opposition winning an election. The others variously came to office by being stand-ins ("caretakers") until a party could elect a new one. That is why we had Page for nineteen days, Forde for seven days and McEwen for twenty-two days. As for finally leaving office, only Menzies resigned at a time of his own choosing. Three died in office, eight were defeated at an election, five were voted out by their party while in office, three knew they were (probably) only caretakers and one was dismissed by the Governor-General. It's interesting to observe that the person we call the Prime Minister is not mentioned in the Commonwealth Constitution. It's simply a convention of the Westminster system of government that one of the ministers commissioned by the Governor-General is called the Prime Minister and is considered the head of our federal government.

Before Federation in 1901 some heads of colonial governments (New South Wales, for example) had the title "Prime Minister", but to avoid confusion once we were one nation they became "premiers", which means the same as "prime ministers". The Constitution that governs the organs of government in this country was a document drawn up by Australians and then enacted by the British Parliament. The British Government wanted some changes and they succeeded in persuading us to accept some very minor ones. One statement still in the Constitution says that the monarch (meaning in effect the British Government) can disallow any Act of the Australian Parliament within two years of its being passed, but that section has been a "dead letter" for at least ninety years, and was never used by the British. We Australian voters can of course change the Constitution if the Parliament presents us with a referendum requiring an answer of "yes" or "no". In most cases so far we have said "no"!

> Sir Robert Menzies once said "Not only do I think everybody in Australia ought to be allowed to say what he thinks about me but, on my experience, everybody does".

Letters to Newspapers and Magazines- the Detail

During the many hours spent in the waiting room of doctors and dentists down the years there was an opportunity to read parts of magazines that I didn't usually read at other times. That included *Time, Newsweek, Readers' Digest, The Bulletin* and *National Geographic*. If the magazine had a "Letters to the Editor" section that was generally my first stopping place. When there was a newspaper at home I read the letters pages from about the age of ten and once I reached my early twenties the desire to become a regular part of the intrepid band of letter writers ("correspondents") grew rapidly.

It was never my practice to write to journals just for the sake of doing so. Some happening or topic of discussion would stir me to write so that my opinion could be read by many. There is disappointment when a letter is sent but not published, but all of us who write understand that that is a natural hazard of the game. Once I retired the volume of letters written increased and thus most of the copies I have kept date from my late fifties.

When my "corresponding career" began letters had to be posted to the newspaper office, unless the writer happened to be close to the newspaper office. I once handed a letter personally to someone in the letters department of *The Sydney Morning Herald*, but otherwise almost all my letters were sent by post. For many years now we have been able to deliver our letters instantaneously, first by facsimile ("fax") and since about the beginning of this century, by email. It makes things much easier than having to get to the post office as quickly as possible and it means that letters are now published while the topic *is* quite topical.

When I first began sending letters to The Sydney Morning Herald the letters published in the paper always began with the ascription "Sir" since the paper's Editor was a man and the letter was ostensibly sent to him. Most of us signed our letters in the form of "D. H. Morrison", if male, or if a woman, in a form such as "(Mrs) S.A. Smith". For many years now it has been plain "David Morrison" or "Sadie Smith".

Most papers and magazines still require letter writers to give their full postal address and a telephone number so that checks of authenticity can be made. For some years someone from the *Herald* would ring letter-writers whose letter was to be published the following morning. There was no promise but a statement that "your letter has been short-listed". One such ringer-up was a man named Ben Willing, a member of the editorial staff. On rare occasions there was a phone call from the office checking on authenticity and on one occasion long ago there was discussion about the wording of the letter. That was in the days when most writers were listed with a phone number and postal address in the White Pages and could have their identity checked, but that sadly is no longer a way of contacting most people.

At this point you will see some examples of my letters, with others interspersed through the book so that the shock of a single hit of letters won't be felt. Since the number of my published letters would be around one thousand you will be relieved to know that only a small minority of those will be repeated in these pages. If I were to include all the *unpublished* letters the number would be in the thousands. Enough already. Some examples follow. The dates given are the dates of publication. The choice of letters, especially those to *The Sydney Morning Herald* and *The Australian*, has been more or less at random. That meant taking a number at random and then choosing a smaller number from those.

The letters chosen have been selected to include a variety of topics, but those topics are only a small number of the total covered by all my letters. Titles given to the letters are in most cases my own, added as I type the letters here. One temptation I have had to avoid while typing is changing the text in an attempt to improve it! What you see is what I wrote, apart from inadvertent typing errors, removal of parentheses that are no longer relevant to the text and very occasional editing by the newspapers' editors.

Until computers took over I wrote letters on a typewriter.

Letters to *The Blue Mountains Gazette*

<u>Should Australia be a republic?</u>　　　　　　　　　　6th July, 1993

The monarchy versus republic debate deserves to be conducted without too much heat and with plenty of light. I would like to make a few points to highlight, with low heat, the conservative side of the argument. We are at present virtually a *de facto* republic with the safeguard of royal and vice-regal conventions built up over many centuries. A declaration of a republic will not necessarily maintain those safeguards.

The Prime Minister [Paul Keating] says he is taking a "minimalist" position, but it is hard to see how such a position can be maintained in reality if we have a major constitutional move away from the Crown. It should also be remembered that this is the Prime Minister who, as Treasurer, campaigned to have a GST introduced [Mr Keating had more recently campaigned hard *against* a GST]. Is he someone who can be trusted to maintain a consistent position?

Some republicans refer back to Sir John Kerr's action in 1975 when he dissolved the parliament and forced the nation to an election. This was in fact democracy at work when the two real villains in the play, Messrs Whitlam and Fraser, were together producing a constitutional crisis. Although his modus operandi may have been questionable, the Queen's representative did the only reasonable thing- give the people the chance to vote in a workable parliament.

Looking back over the past 200 years, republics do not seem to have worked nearly as well as monarchies. This could be the subject of much more investigation.

Finally, one argument used by republicans is that by removing the last vestiges of monarchy we will become more acceptable in Asia. More acceptable with Japan, Malaysia and Thailand, three important monarchies? Actually, that argument hardly supports the contention that Australia has to stand up and assert her independence!

(During the 1990s, until the republic referendum in late 1999, I wrote many letters on the above subject to several newspapers and several were published.)

<u>A silly letter to make a point</u>   mid-1980s

In a recent letter to the Gazette a correspondent referred to the title "relieving master" in a school as a "sexist term". This prompts me to bring into the open a serious situation that exists in my home.

We have a fowl yard with one rooster and several hens (soon to be renamed male and female chookpersons). Whenever the rooster gets annoyed he attacks me (and hurts!). What worries me is that the hens not only look different, they also act differently. Where have I gone wrong in their upbringing? Has the hidden curriculum got to them? (Where did they find it?). Of course they are only birds of ordinary intelligence- called "average lay persons". They could easily be egged on in their sexism. And chooks have no laws to run foul of.

The obvious question in readers' minds is, are the chooks left wing or right wing? There seems to be no special bias in either direction, and in fact they generally have a flutter both ways. I agree that, in general, sexism begins at birth, or even before that. Babies keep insisting being born the female of the species. But what hope is there when we keep using words such as master and mistress, male and female, boy and girl? But-wait a minute- on the other hand...no, no, I must not be reactionary.

<u>Another silly letter to make a point</u>   12th February, 2025

It's indubitably beyond reasonable dispute that ensconcing a multifarious supermarket edifice in Springwood will have a very unpropitious outcome, perhaps a grossly deleterious effect, when it come to the desirability of the town as a location for commerce and socialising.

To put it in words that even developers and government officials can understand, I'll use words of one syllable only. Don't put this big shop in a place where it might, and in fact must, cause the town we love to go down in flames (so to speak) and that may make some of the small and not so small shops that are there now go to the wall, with bad ends for the folk who call this place home and most of whom want it to be a nice place to live for the rest of their lives.

Our funny language   7th December, 2005

The Gazette headline refers to "Back to back wins" for Best Backpacker Accommodation, but the photograph shows the winners facing the camera. A photo of them back to back would have been more interesting. Backpackers back to back would of course be standing pack to pack but whatever their position, congratulations to Blue Mountains YHA.

Our beliefs   22nd December, 2005

Mike Chirgwin says that "theologians and real biblical scholars don't claim that the Bible is the word of God". In the same way it has been said that real men don't eat quiche. It wouldn't be hard to find hundreds of theological graduates (with real degrees) in Australia alone who believe that the Bible is the word of God. A list of the "greats" throughout history who have believed it would take up all the letter space in the Gazette.

An anomaly to an old man   9th June, 2004

I've noticed in recent years the growing practice of people living together as man and wife, perhaps for years, then becoming engaged (still living together) and some time after that getting married. Is that putting the cart before the horse, putting two carts before the horse, putting the horse between two carts, putting a cart between two horses or putting two horses before the cart?

The facts are important   27th April, 2011

Marty O'Neill takes the post-election campaign a step further when he writes that Roza Sage was "not genuinely elected". The Electoral Commission thinks otherwise, as a glance at the scoreboard will indicate.

Cheeky   20th January, 2016

Tony Stephen reminds us that the Gonski education changes will not be fully funded in the way originally announced by Labor. Perhaps that is because Labor forgot that for funding to work there have to be funds.

Let's sit on the verandah and have a break from letters.

The Verandah

Or is it the *veranda*? The word doesn't seem to be used much these days, with *patio* and the old-fashioned *porch* more in favour. It's *beranda* in Malay and Indonesian, which is where we get it from. Did you know that Bahasa Indonesia, the national language of Indonesia, is much the same as Malay, the official tongue of Malaya, the country which later became the larger Malaysia? But all that is beside the point. This little interlude in the story, or rather my miscellany of autobiographically-charged ramblings, is coverage of my sleeping arrangements from the ages of twelve to twenty. And so to bed.

During those mainly teenage years there were at first seven of us in the house, our parents, my brother and sister and our maternal grandmother and our aunt, who was our mother's sister. Grandma and Auntie Muriel were born in 1875 and 1916 respectively . Until I was about sixteen my brother Robert slept at one end of the open verandah at the front of our house at 15 Burns Road, Wahroonga and after that when the two afore-mentioned ladies went to a different domicile he moved to a room with four walls. I continued to sleep at the other end of the verandah, with a large canvas blind that could be rolled down when the weather was not inclement (don't you love that word?). In winter it was usually pretty cool, with morning temperatures down to about five degrees Celsius, but on warm summer evenings I nearly always needed a blanket while those inside had only a sheet as the outside temperature sank well below that in the rooms inside.

Wendy's dog Jock, a part-Scottie, used to sleep under the bed and we were good company. The verandah by the way was at the front of the house and if I "slept in" for a while there was always the likelihood that a visitor would arrive and knock on the door near the foot of the bed. At least they didn't knock on my foot in bed.

…and now back to those letters…

Letters to *The Sydney Morning Herald*

Over three hundred letters have been published in the above paper, the earliest being I think in 1966. Most were written after I retired in 1997. Here are some examples.

<u>Freedom</u>   2nd April, 1971

I was rather surprised and quite annoyed to hear, in a news report, that the NSW Teachers' Federation, of which I am a member, was lobbying the State Government to ensure that the Anti-Discrimination Bill would be effective in outlawing single-sex schools. It is bad enough when the Federation expresses unrepresentative views on such matters as preference for unionists, "sexism" in state schools, examinations and corporal punishment, but at least these are legitimate concerns. It is much worse when, representing tens of thousands of teachers whose views have not been sought, the Federation tries to persuade the legislature to impose its (supposed) views on schools outside the State system.

Many of us in the State system, probably a big majority, would prefer to teach at a "mixed" school. We may be convinced that they are much better, if well supervised and run, than single-sex schools. That surely does not give us the right to dictate our terms to other educational systems. We have had the State

Government's assurance from the start that schools would either by regulation or amendment be exempted from the proposed Act. The public should be assured that the state teachers are not nearly as bigoted and repressive in their attitudes as some Federation officials sometimes indicate.

Religious differences   15th August, 1978

While wishing the Cardinals well as they meet to select their leader [the new Pope], Protestants should remind the community that the issues concerned with belief in the papacy are among the handful of major doctrinal differences which appear to make church union impossible.

In recent years there seems to have developed an attitude that the differences between Protestants and Roman Catholics do not really matter. This is merely pretence, with Protestants being probably the greater pretenders.

The cause of Christian unity can only be correctly served if these fundamental differences are squarely faced. Honest Protestants and honest Roman Catholics know that Protestants cannot accept that the Pope is the successor of St Peter and the Vicar of Christ.

It is also understood by informed people that the whole question of authority (and especially the role of the Bible) poses insurmountable problems unless one side at least makes enormous changes in its fundamental position. Rancour, bitterness and bigotry are not to be desired, but neither are wishy-washy, head-in-the-sand attitudes. With a new Pope in office there will most likely be a surge of interest in ecumenical trends. Let us hope that this will not mean a blunting of clear thought and strong conviction.

The republic debate   22nd October, 1999

Everyone who has followed the referendum debate knows that there are two main groups advocating a "no" vote. There are the monarchists and the "direct electionists" [those who wanted a general election to choose the President]. At the moment they are united in purpose because they both want a better outcome than the model being proposed by the "yes" campaign. If the "no" case wins on November 6, the two groups will again become opponents. The direct electionists will work hard to bring about another referendum and the monarchists will try to ensure we keep our present system. Those who imply that there is something clandestine going on in the "no" campaign show that they have not been paying attention to the published facts.

Branch stacking   26th December, 2000

The Prime Minister [John Howard] is reported as saying that branch stacking is not unwholesome. It is "not" a lot of things. It is not fair, decent or democratic. It is not likely to encourage membership of a political party and it does not help to produce a parliament of true representatives.

Politicians   9th March, 2005

Louise Dodson has highlighted the sad fact that fewer and fewer seem to have political ideals. More of us might be attracted to party loyalty but for the fact that parties tend to love preference deals, branch stacking, opportunism, blowing with the wind and excessive discipline of members. Two of the people I most admired in politics were Tom Uren and Jim Cairns, men with

I disagree ideologically. We could do with more such politicians who believe policy is more important than popularity.

Paying tax regardless   4th October, 2008

If we applied across the board Brad Parry's claim that we shouldn't pay taxes to support anything we don't agree with, it would result in chaos for the Tax Office and tax legislation several hundred pages longer than at present.

Speeding   11th June, 2010

It is always interesting to the complaints coming in when government revenue-raising through speeding fines is highlighted. There is one sure and safe solution to avoiding those voluntary taxes. Those who thumb their noses at the law can hardly complain when they are asked to pay money to the community for the privilege.

The AV (King James) Bible   2nd May, 2011

Four hundred years ago on May 2, 1611, translators published what is known as the Authorised Version, or King James Version, of the Bible. The translation was designed to be read aloud in church services as well as privately at home. For Christians, this anniversary is a celebration of the best-known English translation of the word of God. For everyone who loves the English language, it is a reminder of the contribution the translators made to the English language. Although its old-fashioned language has meant it has been used far less as modern translations have appeared, it is still widely loved and we should be thankful for all the hard work done so long ago.

Naughty boys · 30th August, 2011

The idea of students assessing teachers is not new. During my teaching years, a high school student would sometimes give me a very frank assessment of my performance. The lucidity of the assessment would often result in the student being sent straight to the principal's office to repeat the assessment.

Henry VIII · 7th December, 2011

I assume that Helen Blacklaws is joking when she says that the Protestant faith was a result of Henry VIII's divorce. By the time of the divorce the Reformation under Martin Luther had been well under way in Germany for more than a decade and the young John Calvin, the other great Reformer, was already an active advocate of Protestantism in Europe. Even those who insist on being Anglo-centric must realise that Henry's actions were simply a catalyst for the Reformation which was inevitably coming to England and the rest of Britain.

"Autonomous" cars · 16th January, 2015

In your article "Are we ready for cars with no drivers?" such cars are several times described as "autonomous". Does that mean that these vehicles will make up their own road rules, that is, in common parlance, will they be a law unto themselves?

The **shortest letter** I ever had published anywhere appeared on 14th September, 2013. There had been letters about who should lead the *Herald* Letters Page Party as its chief "power broker". Correspondents were vying to see who could display the greatest brevity when putting himself or herself forward as the leader. My letter was as follows:

I.

That's the "perpendicular pronoun" as the fictional Sir Humphrey called it.

One of the *Herald* letters editors acknowledged it as almost certainly the shortest letter ever published by the paper.

More letters later! (*Oh no! I hear you cry*)

Some Interesting People

The world would be a dull place if we were deprived of some unusual or eccentric people, people who can sometimes be a bit annoying but who are mostly well-meaning and often good companions or conversationists (but not necessarily good conservationists). The people whose names follow have all been deceased for quite some years, up to several decades, at the time of writing, and since it is most unlikely that any of their relatives or friends (other than our family) will read these accounts, it seems safe to mention them by at least their first names.

The first I will mention is Ivy M, an unmarried lady who was in middle age when I first knew her. She was a regular church-going Anglican who might be called a connoisseur of sermons. There were times when she would listen to a sermon outside the church window at Wahroonga and as soon as it was finished she would catch a train two stations away in time hear the sermon at the Anglican church at Turramurra. At least that is what I was told.

Ivy lived with her unmarried sister in the street parallel to ours and the back fence was not far from ours. Miss M was once asked to come down and help my mother in some kind of emergency and she made sure she put her hat on as a display of good manners before coming through the yard at the back of our place. I also remember as a boy being amused when Miss M was taking up Sunday school exam papers we had been answering and as she picked them up she said "Excuse my left hand". I mention these things partly because many members of that generation were very particular about good manners, including the wearing of a hat even when visiting through the back gate in an emergency.

That attitude regarding manners was not of course confined to eccentric or interesting people. Miss M was a kind and good-living lady whose eccentricities were especially noteworthy to us as children and young teenagers. I excuse my writing about people's eccentricities by admitting to the many that I have had. I think Anna's mother found difficulty sometimes in regarding me as "normal" because of my eccentric behaviour at times. Have readers detected that?

Examinations on a Sunday

By the way- did I mention Sunday school exams? They were formal examinations set by the Department of Education of the Anglican Diocese of Sydney and were attempted at many churches on a particular Sunday of the year. One memorable aspect was that there were no time limits on doing the exams, something that can be an advantage for slow writers (or slow thinkers like yours truly). One year my sister Wendy and I decided that we would take as long as possible and keep the supervisors waiting longer than they might have expected. Miss M may have been on duty that year, but my memory fails me there. Naughty children we were, as the reader will no doubt rightly think. But back to the topic of particular people.

An Old Soldier and Others

A man we met late in his life had recently become widowed. Edwin O began attending our church and as an ex-major in the British Army he had fascinating stories of his time serving during the Second World War. I was sorry that I hadn't written down or better still, made a sound recording of his tales, but someone had told him he might be in contravention of the Official Secrets Act if he told too much. I don't see how describing making a pot of tea as the enemy attacked could give secrets to any potential enemy fifty years later, but in any case I left my move too late as he grew older (as we all do! Grow older, I mean). He had come up through the ranks to become a major, unlike the English Public School boys who could go straight into officer training and start their service as an officer. Even in their case of course the rank of major had to wait until they had been a lieutenant and a captain.

Howard P had been active in church circles all his life when I first met him in his senior years. One thing I remember about him was his enthusiastic singing of hymns in church. He had one note and he stuck to it. I have read in two biographies how Sir Marcus Loane, at one time Anglican Archbishop of Sydney, had the same approach to music. He was indeed a man of note. One. Howard ("Mr P..." to us young 'uns!) was a very likeable man and he seemed to find great happiness when he married for the first time in his sixties or seventies.

Almost anyone who has spent much time as a church organist or as a member of church choirs, and who has a sense of humour, can think of many amusing things that happen in those contexts. Members of congregations also notice some of these things. One rare but interesting event is the onset of a power blackout which causes the electricity to the organ and the lights in the church to cease functioning. On one occasion at Wahroonga a light bulb fell from a very high light near the communion table, breaking loudly as it hit the hard floor. The minister leading the service had a smile when he announced the next scheduled hymn, "Lead kindly light".

For a while we had at our church in Wahroonga an organist, Mr A, who seemed to pounce on the keyboard. He played in an organ loft and beside him was a light that cast a large shadow of the organist on the wall next to the choir. Some of the gathered people could see the big shadow pounce as it played. He once told some choir members that he went surfing before church and with water in his ears he sometimes couldn't hear the minister announcing the next hymn. It's interesting that a number of organists around the world over the years have died either at the keyboard or very soon after playing. That doesn't make it qualify as a hazardous occupation and therefore danger money is not paid.

John Cowland

Captain John Cowland was a man whom I met after his retirement. He had come to Australia from England in 1931 and started the official Church Army in Australia. There had been a bit of Church Army activity in south-eastern Australia up to 1903, but it was apparently not very significant compared to the later movement. Captain Cowland's first wife had died and around the time of his retirement he married his former secretary who was now Mrs Maude Cowland. They were a very pleasant couple to have home for dinner and conversation. The Captain tried to persuade me to join the Church Army, which was a bit like the Salvation Army in some ways, but very much Anglican. In 2023 the Church Army of Australia held its final meeting before its activities were wound up for ever (?) and since it was held only a few kilometres from our place it was easy for me to attend. My memory of the Captain is summarised in a letter that I wrote to the Sydney Anglican journal Southern Cross in that 2023.

Letter about John Cowland

It was very surprising to read the article in the May-June edition of Southern Cross on the end times of the Church Army in Australia without seeing any reference to Captain John Cowland. He was the English clergyman who founded the Church Army in Australia in the early 1930s and led it for years afterwards.

I came to know Captain Cowland in the late 1950s after his retirement, when he acted as least twice as locum at St Andrew's, Wahroonga. He had obviously been a force to reckon with and was still a powerful preacher. He could summon a very loud voice, whether he was preaching or singing.

On at least one occasion during his ministry he was confronted with prisoners who refused to keep quiet as he stood to give his sermon. He said in a very loud voice "You can all go to hell!" A stunned silence ensued and then he completed the sentence with "but you don't have to". He then continued with his sermon.

He was a bit too "high church" and non-Reformed for my taste, not an evangelical but a good evangelist. I believe that many came into the Kingdom of God because of him and his co-workers. He should be remembered by name in any account of the Church Army of Australia.

And now- just ahead are *more* letters to newspapers, as promised!

Letters to *The Australian*

<u>Introduction</u>- Nearly all my letters to The Australian were written from 2015 onwards when I changed my full subscription to that paper instead of *The Sydney Morning Herald*. It seemed to me that by the time the latter paper had changed from a broadsheet to a tabloid it had lost some of its gravitas and was too intolerant of those of a conservative political bent (such as I!). The Herald retained some features not found in *The Australian,* such as *Column 8* and a cryptic crossword that I can usually do- unlike the ones in some papers. I continued to write an occasional letter but *The Australian* became my main focus, with only an intermittent online subscription to the *Herald*. According to my count I have had about 300 published letters in the Australian. Here are some of them.

<u>Language oppression</u>　　　　　　　　12th May, 2015

Reading the editorial on political correctness in universities reminded of an essay I wrote a few years ago. I wrote "mankind" to see what would happen. Sure enough, the marker put a red ring around the word. Political correctness is an obsession at many universities.

<u>"Quotas" in politics</u>　　　　　　　　6th August, 2016

It's probably a long time before the next federal election, but there is one aspect that should be looked at as soon as possible.

Labor policy is to have at least 50 per cent women as its MPs within 10 years. The Greens have a 50 per cent target and many Liberals are pushing for the same. The Labor policy is the most obviously sexist because it means there is no limit to the proportion of women, but men are to have a permanent limit of 50 per cent.

One problem is that so many activists misuse the idea of representation when they say that women should have more representation in parliaments. A recently-elected Liberal female [I wrote "woman"] MP was asked how she would represent women in the House. Her reply was that she was elected to represent everyone in her electorate. I have no objection to being represented for the past six years by four different women at state and federal level, two from the Coalition and two from Labor, but the idea of quotas is undemocratic.

(The above letter is as slightly altered by the letters editors. "Recently elected" referred to a woman who had been recently elected in a 1960s election!)

<u>Marriage</u>   7th September, 2016

Sophie York asks whether those of us who believe in the current definition of marriage will be free to promulgate our views if same-sex marriage is recognised by law. The answer must be a resounding yes. Otherwise, those who are making assurances that such a change will have no effect on the rest of us are simply trying to charm us with empty words.

Christianity and society — 14th September, 2016

To be fair, Peter McLeod-Miller must admit that during the past few centuries, Christianity has had a positive effect on such social questions as the abolition of slavery, respect for women, the dignity of children, freedom of speech and association, and tolerance for different religions and ethnic groups.

Blokes — 18th-19th February, 2017

John Bain's idea of a Blokes International group sounds good to me. I might join and become one of its powerbrokers.

The Senate — 2nd February, 2017

I think the Senate has a very valuable function and a referendum to abolish it would probably fail. A better idea might be to ask the people to approve a limit on the Senate's ability to delay any money bill originating in the lower house. A six-month delay would not stop the government from governing but would give time to scrutinise legislation.

(The above was somewhat edited by the paper.)

The Gospel story — 10th October, 2017

Peter Fleming might have added that the only charge against Jesus the temple authorities could make stick was that he claimed to be God. The Roman governor could find no fault in him, but for the sake of peace he did the accusers' bidding and had him executed. That Jesus was punished although innocent of any wrongdoing is a vital aspect of Christian theology.

The group called "GetUp"   21st November, 2018

The most objectionable thing about the group called GetUp is its operatives at polling booths telling voters they are not recommending a vote for any party. They then say "put the Liberals last", which makes the vote effectively one for Labor. Honesty is apparently not for them the best policy.

Freedom   3rd September, 2019

I fear that the federal government's proposed legislation on religious freedom will only complicate matters and be a hindrance rather than a help towards freedom. What we need is a society where goodwill and fairness are part of all our dealings and where freedom is assumed and practised. The main issue is freedom, not just religious freedom. The idea of the government in a democratic nation having to legislate to give us basic freedoms sends a chill down the spine.

Malcolm Turnbull   5th November, 2021

Despite the man's undoubted talent and intellect, I was a bit cranky when John Howard encouraged Malcolm Turnbull to enter parliament. I vowed never to vote Liberal if he were the leader of the party, and I still feel the pain of voting for Bill Shorten. What really astounded me was that after removing Mr Turnbull as leader of the opposition, the party later made him PM.

Climate   25th October, 2022

Anna O'Hara says we should give our climate a sporting chance. Our national climate, with its captain Al Nino and vice-captain La Nina, seems to play a pretty hard game and doesn't look like succumbing to the opposition.

Real debate   8th August, 2023

G K Chesterton could have been watching Q&A or similar programmes if the year 1910 didn't pinpoint his comment in time. Referring to the importance of debate, he wrote, "The really burning enthusiast never interrupts, he listens to the enemy's arguments as easily as a spy would listen to the enemy's arguments". He commented that genuine, fair "cut and thrust" had become "very rare". I can't help wondering how he would react to today's Dorothy Dixers and the refusal to answer questions in our parliaments.

Choosing judges   12th September, 2023

In my opinion the only really good reason for deliberately choosing a woman as a judge is to put her there a role model for girls. The Solicitor-General of WA apparently believes that "diversity" should trump outstanding ability in choosing members of the judiciary where there is a "diverse" candidate for the job. Most of us ordinary people would prefer the authorities to appoint judges who are tops on ability, integrity and experience. Sometimes those people will be women. The Solicitor-General seems to be implying that normal processes won't bring many forward. Feminists may conclude that he has some questions to answer.

Our way of life   21ˢᵗ November, 2023

Nick Cater reports that only 40 per cent of Australians believe it's important to support Australia's culture and way of life. That is indeed a depressing figure if it refers to fairness, mateship, discussion of differences without animosity, the rule of law, tolerance without surrender to the woke, a sound parliamentary system, incorruptible police forces, promotion on merit and so on.

If, however, it refers to the Australia increasingly realised by the woke, including many in the ABC and radical politicians on the left, perhaps it's good if only a minority looks forward to the continuation of that kind of Australia. It may be a vain hope but it would be wonderful if most of our people looked at the good things that have occurred in our history and genuinely tried to continue and improve on those. Those who try to ruin our way of life by continued negativity about our past, our Constitution, our institutions, our tolerance and our sense of "live and let live" ought to be ashamed of themselves.

Teaching what we believe   23ʳᵈ May, 2024

It's a strange world. Some parents complain that a teacher visiting Catholic schools will teach Catholics values on sexuality, and the schools cave in. It seems axiomatic that people sending their children to church schools or independent Christian schools expect them to be taught Christian morality. Parents who don't want that can save money by opting for state schools where, they will be pleased to find, Christian values on sexuality are no longer taught.

<u>Writing speeches</u>　　　　　　　　　　　　7th June, 2024

If I were a minister forced to give a speech on "the multifarious manifestations of the disincentives inherent in the distribution of rubber mats", knowing that almost no one would listen to or read the speech, I might consider having it written by a public servant. Otherwise, for key speeches, I don't see why an educated and responsible minister can't write (or just speak) his or her own composition.

<u>The Dismissal</u>　　　　　　　　　　　　6th August, 2024

Greg Craven refers to Gough Whitlam's dismissal as a constitutional crisis. The fact is that whatever we think of Sir John Kerr's part in the drama, his action was the deed that ended the crisis.

That completes my selection of letters from three newspapers, one local weekly, one metropolitan daily and one national daily.

Don't worry. There are more to come later from smaller-circulation papers!

In 2018 there was a mention in the paper of a letter written to The Times in London by Jonathan Lynn, one of the two script writers of the television series Yes, Minister and Yes, Prime Minister. He quoted Sir Humphrey Appleby's words in one episode when he should have attributed the words to Mr Hacker, the Prime Minister. The sentence quoted was "The first rule of politics: never believe anything till it's officially denied". I sent an email correcting the mistake and Jonathyn Lynn replied "Many thanks for the correction. I am truly impressed. You know my work much better than I know it myself, and your memory is clearly a lot better than mine. Thank you for your kind words. I will not mistakenly attribute that quotation in future."

English usage

Languages change constantly. It is therefore a bit presumptuous (don't you love big words?) to be prescriptive about what is right and wrong in grammar and other aspects of the spoken and written word. It is preferable to use terms such as "good" and "bad" when referring to usage, or perhaps "felicitous" and "not felicitous" (!). Despite the hazards, I will jot down some of my pet dislikes in the way English is used, in the interests of clear communication and having words say what they actually mean.

I will give examples that I believe are against the spirit of good English and explain why I think it should be expressed differently. Some of the following "transgressions" are relative newcomers to the language (the use of "including" being one example) and others have been with us far too long (such as people saying "is" when they mean "are").

Sit back and observe a pedant at work. Pedants have to live with the hazard that they will sometimes be caught out by other pedants or those who look to dismantle pedantry. But being a pedant can still be fun.

Many are sick, including in their homes. No. Many are sick, including people in their homes.

Jim sat the exam. No. Jim sat **for** the exam. He sat down and did the exam.

There's many people there. No. There **are** many people here.

He played football on back-to-back weekends. That's too funny to need comment.

I like pies, lollies and cakes, etc. There's nothing wrong with that as written, but most people say "ekk settra" instead of "ett settra". The expression of course is a Latin phrase, *et cetera*, which means "and other things".

You better eat that food. No. You **had** better eat that food.

He was laying on the ground. Well- some dialects do say it like that, but good usage in printed English would tell us he was **lying** on the ground.

*The company should do well, **going forward**.* That is not good English- why not use a normal phrase such as *in the future* or *from now on*?

And a more recent barbarism is the use of *absent* in in strange way. *Absent a thunder storm, it should be a completely fine day.* No! *In the absence of* a storm, it should be a completely fine day.

Other "interesting" uses of language

The programme will be on at the special time of 8:00 pm. That usually means that it will be at a different time, whether convenient to the viewer or not.

We're not advising you how to vote, but put the …. party last. That *is* advising us how to vote! But enough of my pedantry!! I could go on page after page after page and bore the reader silly.

Genuine Composition

This book has been written by me. I believe that people who claim to be the author of something should be the actual author. That's why I don't like the practice of writing speeches for politicians and others, unless they acknowledge that they didn't write them. It's even worse when written articles are written by "ghost" writers with no hint given that the supposed author had little to do with the actual composition. Imagine if it could be proved that Shakespeare's plays were written by team of writers with Bill himself giving only a bit of input here and there.

Apparently Winston Churchill had only one speech written for him (a boring speech on economics) but in the event he didn't actually give it. It is of course interesting to notice that the writing of speeches for someone else to give goes back to ancient times. By contrast, Robert Gordon Menzies, later Sir Robert, wrote in the 1930s his views that speakers in general should compose their speeches as they went, exceptions being such occasions as a Minister of the Crown making an important official statement.

An English actor some years ago was asked by a publisher to write his autobiography. The publisher told him to write a certain number of pages and they would then decide if he might write the book or whether the actual task would be given to a helper. Once he had written the required number of pages he was told that they were good enough and that he could go on writing the book himself. His comment was that, if the publisher had said he wasn't permitted to write it, that would have been the end of the endeavour and the book would not have been written.

What could (and should) have been an embarrassing incident happened when Dr Martyn Lloyd-Jones, perhaps the greatest preacher in Britain in the twentieth century, was on holidays. He attended an Anglican church *incognito* and was rather surprised when the minister preached one of the Doctor's printed sermons, without admitting that he was preaching someone else's sermon. The only way the Anglican preacher would find out that the author had heard him reading his own words would be by reading about it years later in Iain Murray's excellent biography of Dr Lloyd-Jones.

I do find it disturbing to realise that many quoted speeches and parts of speeches, including pithy sayings, even speeches by great men and women, are not the actual creations of those who spoke them. It is valid for speakers to read compositions of other people in some circumstances but the pretence that words are one's own, when they are not, is to be lamented. At least, that is my view.

Time to Eat

This section should be headed "nomenclature regarding meal and snack times" but it's not so catchy a title. During my life there have appeared various words to denote a particular eating and/or drinking experience at different times of day, including breakfast, brunch, lunch, dinner, tea, morning tea and afternoon tea. The one that causes the most confusion in Australia is probably *dinner*, followed by *tea*, especially in the latter case by immigrants or visitors from Britain.

In my experience people from rural areas tend to call the midday meal *dinner*, whereas to me dinner is the evening meal except on special occasions such as Christmas Day, when it is nearly always in the middle of the day. As for *tea*, the word can mean the evening meal or afternoon tea, with or without food (usually with). On one occasion we invited an English-born man to "tea", meaning the evening meal. He arrived in mid-afternoon and after some afternoon tea he was surprised when we told him we expected him to stay for the evening meal- what we had meant by "tea".

When I was a boy my brother Robert and I were staying at the country home of Uncle Charlie and Auntie Hazel Bayliss. One afternoon their son John and I were playing some distance from the house and Auntie Hazel called out "would you boys like some lunch?" We had already had our midday meal and I queried John as to her meaning. His reply was "she means afternoon tea".

Flora and fauna

Back in the early1980s George Henry (see later) and his cousin Flora Morrison were visiting the zoo in Sydney. Auntie Flora told me later that George was a difficult man to be with in that setting because as an ornithologist and naturalist he was interested in examining birds and some other creatures closely. He would stop at each cage or showcase for quite some time while Auntie flora "cooled her heels" and became tired standing at each spot. It occurred to me years later that it was interesting that while George was inspecting fauna he was accompanied by Flora. Well, I have to fill this book up somehow.

Fashion

One thing among many others than has intrigued me through much of my life has been the idea of things and ideas being in or out of fashion. With things that can easily change it is perhaps understandable, but it doesn't make much sense with things that don't usually change over short periods of time. When someone says that planting a particular kind of shrub is in fashion it makes me wonder if it will still be "in fashion" when it reaches a mature size and has the full look of its species. If it's a tree it may have to stay in fashion for a lifetime if fashion is particularly important to people.

Some years ago I read that splayds were then virtually unused simply because they had gone out of fashion. I don't eat at many people's places and that means it's not possible to observe how widely splayds are now used. At our place they are used from time to time, perhaps once a fortnight when we are eating from a bowl rather than the usual plate. They are certainly neither in or out of fashion with us- we just use them when it's convenient to do so. If hammers go out of fashion and people start hitting nails with the end of spanners I shall still use a hammer, fashionable or not. Just for fun I Googled "splayds" as I was composing this paragraph and it is clear that a number of big well-known stores still sell them in 2025.

Vertical grills were to my mind a thing of the past at the time of writing, but I notice to my surprise that they are still to be bought. We got rid of ours about forty years ago and rarely used them while we had them. They were popular wedding gifts in days of long ago. Yesteryear, as we used to say. Beards and particular hairstyles are other examples of fashion, although I have often said that my hair style has stayed much the same since I was about five and I have never let my whiskers grow for more than three or four days before shaving them- even during COVID lockdowns. Clothing fashions are of course always changing, and there I have succumbed somewhat, but not completely. I suppose the main thing is not to be a slave of fashion.

One thing I noticed as a teacher was the definite in-and-out-of-fashion nature of yo-yos. For a few weeks they would be prolific in the playground and the teacher on playground duty would often feel obliged to have a go with or without the skill to do a "round the world" yo with the yo-yo. Marbles were another example of playground activity and I was amazed at Goodooga to observe how skilful some Aboriginal children were at the game.

Back to the early years Fire!!

When I was about six months old our house in Wahroonga burnt down. I believe we had to be accommodated at my grandparents' house in Lindfield. The house was rebuilt with some bits of the old one included in the rebuild. Auntie Cath, mentioned with interest elsewhere in this book, sold the house and land to my father and he paid her back little by little over the years. Very late in her life she forgave him the considerable debt remaining and he had some years debt free for about the last ten years of his life.

I remember years after that fire that there was a time when Auntie Hazel, my mother's sister-in-law, was staying with us and lit a fire in the lounge room grate with a large quantity of wood. The chimney caught fire and the fire brigade came, but no damage was done. What I remember most was the roar in the chimney, but that was nothing compared to the roar of a bushfire passing by, as we have known in Springwood.

Colours

When I was young the names of the days of the week and months of the year had colours, or so my mind saw. Numerals also had colours. Although the colours have dimmed somewhat over the years, they are still there at times. When I think if the word "February" in my mind I see the letters in black, while "March" has a subdued red colour. The numeral six is silvery and two is greenish. "Monday" is reddish and "Thursday" is a sort of silvery off-white. At least those are the colours as I write this. Weird, isn't it?!

Some examples of repartee by Sir Robert Menzies and Sir Winston Churchill:

Menzies:

A Miner: "Tell us all you know, Bob-it won't take long!"
Menzies: "I'll tell you all we both know- it won't take any longer."

A Burly Man: "And now tell us the story of The Three Bears."
Menzies: "Certainly I'd like to tell you the story of The Three Bears, but I can't see the other two."

A voice: "Watcha gonna do about 'ousing?"
Menzies: "Put an 'h' in front of it."

At a meeting in London each speaker began, "Your Royal Highness, Your Excellencies, My Lord Archbishop, Your Grace, My

Lords, Your Honours, My Lord Mayor, Your Worships, distinguished guests and gentlemen..." When Menzies got up to speak he said, "Princes, potentates and commoners..."

When Menzies first became Prime Minister in 1939 a Labor man said, "I take it that, before choosing your cabinet, you will consult the powerful interests that control you." Menzies replied "Yes. But please keep my wife's name out of this."

Menzies was very good at thinking on his feet with repartee, while Churchill drew on his capacious memory and reproduced witticisms that he had heard or read over the years.

Churchill:

Lady Astor: "Mr Churchill, if you were my husband I'd give you poison".
Churchill: "Madam, if I were you husband, I'd drink it!"
(There is some doubt about the authenticity of this quotation but I'll use it anyway.)

People I have observed

Stephen Leacock was an academic economist but he is remembered much more for his humorous writings. He lived from 1869 to 1944. In a book called *Short Circuits*, published in 1928, he wrote a collection of essays. Four of these were under a general heading "People we know". I take up this theme nearly a century later and tell tales of some real people who have come into my line of sight and hearing over the years. Each person mentioned may in fact be the representative of more than one person with the same or similar characteristics. In some cases the reference is to specific individuals.

One interesting observation made by Leacock is that sometimes the Man in the Train (or Bus), for example, is at some stage joined by another Man who gets in and causes trouble when he arrives on the scene. One of his best essays in my opinion is about *The Man in the Pullman Car* (that is, the railway carriage). Let's get going with a couple of my observations.

The man who claps first (and it's usually a man)

He can sit anywhere in the auditorium. He usually seems to be well away from where I'm sitting and that gives him a sort of mystique because I know he's there but I'm not sure which particular figure is his. Maybe I had better use this opportunity to confess that there have been occasions when he has been identified, but perhaps I had better not reveal who he is. He would not sue me because he is too decent for that, but we must not take advantage of his good nature and blow his cloak of anonymity. Very occasionally he is a woman, but nearly always a man, in my experience.

When he is at a music performance he generally waits until near the end of a piece or a movement and gives a loud clap at about the beginning of the last bar, although that is quite variable. But he gets in first! He is of course a helpful character when the music is very modern and when no one is quite sure whether or an item is finished and he, with courage, breaks the applause ice. His bravery in clapping first is then much appreciated by audience and musicians alike. He is at his worst when a song finishes and there are a couple of lines of instrumental music still to go. He claps when the words finish and, with those who join him, tries to drown out the last bars of the music. In all this I speak of course of classical music performances. Of other types of performance I know very little. Shame on me, did you say?

When the event is not a musical one he can be a bit of a nuisance. At a Christian conference a speaker finishes a talk with the expectation that the listeners will sit quietly and think about what has been said, but our Man decides to give a clap. Like an infection the clap spreads rapidly to other clappers, sometimes dying down very quickly. At other times a speaker of any kind may say something banal or even cringeworthy and our Man decides that applause is called for when it's definitely not, at least in the eyes (and ears) of most of the audience. But we'll leave him there and hope than one day perhaps he may be too clapped out to clap. At least, not first.

The Man on the Bus

This refers to a number of people I have encountered in my lifetime but it is enshrined in two men in particular, one on a bus from Sydney to Canberra and another from Cootamundra to Griffith. The man who travelled to Canberra was on a bus that took me from Sydney to Perth, a trip that took most of three full daytimes with two nights in between. The relief I felt when he told me he was going only as far as Canberra was enormous. If he hadn't got off at Canberra I think I would have. Putting the two men together, the brief story begins.

He enters the bus and looks around. He espies me with a vacant seat beside me and my heart sinks. "Hello" he says with a smile and sits down. "What do you think of the performance of the Prime Minister lately?" he asks. "Well, he has had…" I reply. Then the Man is off. At least I don't have to say much for the next couple of hours. When I do open my mouth it has to be to agree with him or be regaled by the forty-five reasons why I'm wrong. By that time of course the Prime Minister has been forgotten and I'm listening to details of the Man's childhood or the time he bought paint of the wrong colour or why his car has a back door that jams when it's cold. It time for a rest and I say "Oh, I'm tired. It's time for a bit of a rest".

I close my eyes but while they are closed there is sense of eyes peering at me, waiting for the least sign of stirring. Just before I started my rest he offered me a piece of fruit cake and it was very tempting to ask why I should accept fruitcake from a "fruitcake". In the case of one manifestation of the Man I was parted from him at Canberra, as already noted, while the other one told me several times that he was getting off at Griffith and waiting for some unknown form of transport to take him to some other town to the north. For all I know he is still waiting there, but I'm sure he hasn't been lost for words. I carried on in peace to my destination of Mildura.

I could add the man in the train to my story, just to give some balance to transport modes. There was a young man who sat with me (he in his wrong seat) from Armidale to Tamworth. His self-imposed brief was to tell me in detail his proposal for something or other somewhere or other at some time or other. I was never more glad to see Tamworth station.

The Railway Enthusiast

He turns up especially at those times when a steam locomotive is taken on to the mainline tracks to give pleasure to the nostalgic and glee to the railway enthusiast. Some would say that I am confusing fanaticism with enthusiasm but that may be a bit unfair. On the other hand we must distinguish between the ordinary enthusiast with the enthusiastic enthusiast. The ordinary enthusiast may include those who simply enjoy a day out on an old train for various reasons but who don't take the occasion too seriously. The person I'm talking about the is the *serious* enthusiast. And boy oh boy, can he be serious!

I remember on one occasion in 1970 a relative and his son (who was also my relative!) were in a carriage pulled by a steam train and which was to take us from Central Station in Sydney to Wollongong and back, a round trip of about 160 kilometres. The son was a real enthusiast. We were sitting in a compartment and the father began to ask some questions about the train, including the locomotive. There were others who could hear what was being said and the son was clearly embarrassed with having such an ignorant father in such an important place. At last he leaned over and said quietly in his father's ear "Dad, just pretend you know everything".

My love for all things trains is of course pretty great. My love for steam trains is even greater, but I don't think I qualify as a serious enthusiast, partly because my technical knowledge is not great, but also because I can see the humorous side of railway enthusiasm. On the trip mentioned above, by the time we arrived in Wollongong I was getting a bit sick of nothing but intricate details of locomotives, carriage and tracks by all those around me. As we arrived we could see some double-decker buses which we knew were to take us to a spot for lunch where there would be a display of working model trains. I asked someone next to me whether the buses were steam buses and he- a serious enthusiast- explained carefully and seriously that he thought not. They were probably petrol or diesel buses. Fortunately he didn't detect my naughtiness. Perhaps he was just humouring me!

That was one of many steam trips I and other family members have taken since steam trains were largely taken off mainline running by about 1970. The same father, with the same son, drove me to Newcastle north of Sydney on the day when the last steam-hauled Newcastle Flyer was scheduled to travel from Newcastle to Sydney. We saw the "38 Class" engine being fired up in the Newcastle roundhouse but through poor calculation we missed seeing it as it sped towards Sydney. Apparently there were a couple more uses of steam after that official "last" trip. One important accoutrement, by the way, for many serious enthusiasts is a cap of the sort generally worn by drivers or guards in a past era. Sometimes a train excursion brings to the fore other garments of a railway nature.

In April 1974 I saw a triple-header steam train pass through Springwood. It was announced as the last steam train to do main line trips since the new man in charge of the railways thought they gave the railways an undesirable old-fashioned look. Fortunately that absurd attitude was not widely shared and over fifty years later we still have steam trains plying main lines from time to time.

I'll mention one more thing that happened on that Wollongong trip. On such trips most people want to take photos. At one point the train stopped and we all got out. The train backed up a couple of hundred metres and then charged towards us at full acceleration, puffing out enormous quantities of black smoke while we pointed our cameras and took shots of the phenomenon.

As the train passed we were all showered with particles of coal or soot- black particles.

My biggest regret that day was that in the morning I had put on a white shirt and white shorts.

Fireworks

In my teenage years I had a very rudimentary chemistry laboratory in our garage in Wahroonga, a place never used for a car in my memory and a place we called simply "the shed". One of my favourite little activities was putting aluminium foil into a caustic soda solution and making hydrogen. So long as I waited until all the oxygen was expelled from the flask before lighting the gas as it came out of a narrow tube, all was well. On one occasion I didn't wait and my parents in the house heard a bang. No harm was done but I learnt a lesson, just as I learned another one in high school when I washed out with water a tube with some concentrated acid still in it- sulphuric, I think. It made me jump and the teacher sat us all down and used me as moral for the class. I also learnt that nitric acid takes the skin off the fingers and dissolves clothing it spills on to.

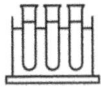

On one Saturday my brother was going to a party where the invitees were asked to bring fireworks. He didn't have any and so we decided to make some ourselves. We used recipes from a magazine called *Hobbies Junior*, a companion journal to *Hobbies Illustrated*. We knew that a year or two earlier a girl had been killed and her brother injured when they were using those same recipes. We also knew that those unfortunate people had been grinding two different chemicals together, something one never does, especially if one of the chemicals when mixed has explosive potential. We found out that adding caster sugar to a firework mixture causes it to burn slowly, allowing the colours caused by combustion to last for a while instead of just going off in a flash.

In those days it was legal to buy and use fireworks. Until sometime in the 1960s we used to have a half-holiday, from midday onwards, to celebrate Empire Day, later Commonwealth Day, held on 24th May, Queen Victoria's birthday. In the evening we would let off fireworks in the yard, including "double bungers", gunpowder-filled small cylinders of cardboard. They made quite a bang and could be dangerous if not thrown from the body once the fuse was lit. We also had smaller bungers and tiny ones that we called "squibs". Later the Queen's official birthday in June was "cracker night" as many called it. In some states the main cracker night was Guy Fawkes' Day, 5th November. My dear readers can catch up on Guy's significance in a relevant history book.

Letters again.
(How many more, you ask?!)

As well as letters to one national, one metropolitan and one local newspaper, some examples of which you have already read, or skimmed over, I have written to a number of other publications. The Sydney Morning Herald gets another mention, but first here are some examples written to a variety of journals.

<u>Letter to *The Penrith Press*</u>　　　　　　　　14th December, 1999

<u>Honesty</u>

I hope the gentleman who handed my wallet in to the ticket office at Penrith station om October 29 reads this. I would like to thank you very much for your thoughtfulness and honesty. What that man did we should do for everyone. But, unfortunately, we know there are far too many dishonest and thoughtless people out there.

Letter to *The Briefing* 2nd July, 1998

Agreeing

It is always good to receive *The Briefing* and to be confident that the subjects treated will be put to the test of Scripture. We may not always agree with every article in every detail, but there is always the assurance that the unique inspiration of the Bible is taken as given.

It is especially encouraging to see the treatment given to topics such as the ministry of women. So often in other publications an unbiblical stance is taken or the writer is too apologetic about his or her attempts to be biblical.

Editors' response to a letter of mine in the *Newsletter* of the Geographical Society of NSW in May, 1993.

An interesting letter was received from one of our members, David Morrison, concerning the day which should be identified as the first day of the new century. The Editor discussed this issue with a number of people and the letter has been included for the benefit of members. The first day of the twentieth century was the 1st January, 1901 and that for the twenty-first century will be the 1st January, 2001.

Don Biddle, Editor   Colin Sale, Associate Editor

Letter to *Eternity* magazine

Women's troubles November, 2014

Dear Sir (as we wrote in more formal days).

According to Greg Clarke, October *Eternity*, "Women report almost universally a sense of being devalued, discredited, sexualised and ignored from an early age". Adding to that extraordinary statement, we are told that things get worse as adolescence sets in, male negativity shapes their image and that most of life is a struggle "just to keep your head above water in a male-dominated world'".

Looking back at about 70 years of memories, I have been acquainted with hundreds of women from many different backgrounds and involved in many paid and unpaid occupations. Some were born in the 19th century. Hundreds of today's women were the girls I taught from kindergarten to Year 12. There are countless "successful" women who are publicly known, including journalists, political activists and leaders, professionals and sportswomen, many of whom impress us and influence us.

From my limited perspective there is no doubt that Greg Clarke's assertions are at best gross exaggerations. Such statement do not help in in a rational assessment of the problems that far too many women still endure in the world.

Letters to *The Canberra Times*

The crucifixion   4th January, 2013

Doug Hind tells us that Jesus was killed by the Romans because Rome did not like his political ideas. That claim could hardly be more wrong. Jesus was killed by the Romans on behalf of the Jews who were offended by Jesus' claim to be God. The Roman governor found no fault with the man and tried to persuade the Jews to have Barabbas, a real lawbreaker, executed [instead].

Letter to *The Canberra Times*

The monarchy   16th January, 2010

Marie Gordon says that "the monarchy is dead in the water and has been for yonks". If that is so it is certainly a corpse with a strong constitution.

The following two letters were published in *The Sydney Morning Herald*, but not on the normal letters page.

28th February, 1999

1. Perhaps the perception of Melbourne being wetter than Sydney comes from the fact that Melbourne has an average of 44 rain days in winter, while Sydney has only 34. Or that Melbourne has an average 48 clear days per year, while Sydney has 87.

1st November, 2003

2. John Paton, who won the VC in the Indian Mutiny in 1857 (and later became governor of Goulburn Gaol), told my uncle that he saw men on overnight marches actually sound asleep as they marched.

At one stage in the 1980s the Sydney Morning Herald had a weekly page called "Commonroom" (it should be two words) where educational ideas were discussed. In those days I was a bit of an activist in the cause of teaching Geography in high schools and I was particularly stirred when History was to be made compulsory in some high school years while Geography was not. On one occasion the Principal called me out of my classroom to tell me that a senior politician who was outside the classroom wanted to discuss the matter with me. I wrote to "Commonroom" and put forward some ideas on the topic. I reproduce it in full as it gives an idea of my thinking more than forty years go as I write.

<u>Letter to "Commonroom"</u>   8th September, 1981

The article on children's rights included the following words of Mr Paul Jeremy: "Kids today feel that so much of school is irrelevant. For example, one might find more value in doing motor mechanics than geography."

What is meant by "more value"? Money? As a teacher of geography I would like to put a case for my subject, very briefly.

Our society makes it compulsory for all to vote at elections, thereby implying that we all have considerable responsibility as citizens. If citizens are to make choices between political parties there needs to be some understanding of major issues such as the use of natural resources, urban and regional development, conservation, foreign policy, the basis of electoral distribution, and a number of other topics which courses in geography deal with to varying degrees.

The main argument concerning relevance in school subjects seems to involve a conflict between true relevance and perceived relevance. It is true that a subject will have much more meaning if a student enjoys it and can see its usefulness, but there is a strong case for teaching subjects which adults know are relevant while at the same time taking pains to convince the students of the fact. We make English, mathematics and science compulsory. Is geography any less relevant to the average student than the second and third subjects in this list?

Geography is a subject which helps students to be more useful citizens by increasing their awareness of the way things come together to form the patterns on the earth's surface. In an increasingly crowded world, it is vital for all of us to have more understanding of man's use of horizontal space. This has at least as much relevance as motor mechanics, even to a motor mechanic. Perhaps in this regard we should give more consideration to student's present and future duties rather than an unbalanced view of "rights".

Geography is an excellent multi-disciplinary subject, involving at times English, mathematics, physics, chemistry, history and more, as well as a large range of concepts and skills that are specifically geographical. I believe that both geography and history should be compulsory to the end of Year 10. To be faced with the choice of one or the other is like being given the choice between eyes and ears.

(I sound like a politician of the Geography Party! The Professor of Geography at The University of New England in NSW wrote a letter starting with "Congratulations on your letter to the Sydney Morning Herald".)

Letter to *New Life*   3rd June, 1999

Kathy MacKendrick can add the Astronomer Royal to the list of people who recognised when the new century and millennium begin. The date is particularly important to Australia. I understand that our founding fathers deliberately chose 1st January 1901 as the date when Australia became one nation because it was the first day of this century.

Letter to *New Life*   8th March, 1990

A few days ago while looking at our innumerable books, some printed last century and one the century before, I came across Paul White's <u>Doctor of Tanganyika</u>, apparently his first "jungle book". Having read a number of his later books many years ago, and having heard him speak in the 1940s and since, it was interesting to see your article on Dr White a couple of days later.

An indication of the popularity of the stories from Africa right from the start is the fact that my copy, published in 1943, is the seventh edition. This appeared 23 months after the first edition! The gripping nature of the narrative explains why the book was so quickly appreciated.

Our children have enjoyed Jungle Doctor stories being read to them and they are certain to be popular for many years yet. Dr White is one of the great evangelical leaders who have been a great strength to the Anglican denomination in Sydney over the last forty years, and whose influence has spread to a much wider world. We can so easily forget to thank God for blessings such as these.

(This letter was signed "D. H. Morrison" but by the end of the century it was always "David Morrison")

Letter to *Education* 6th June, 2003

In replying to Craig Smith's letter the Editor says that Federation [the NSW Teachers' Federation- the Union] was against the war in Iraq because the democratically elected Federation Council said so. I am sure that Mr Howard would likewise say that Australia was in favour of the war because our democratically government said so. The chief difference is that military matters are part of the role of the Federal Government whereas our Federation is supposed to represent its members in relation to educational matters.

<u>Letter to *Southern Cross*</u>   February, 2015

> I had a bit of a chuckle when I read about the busy schedule of the choir at St Andrew's Cathedral over the Christmas period. Ove the past decade or so several people have told me that Philip Jensen abolished the choir when he took office. It must have been very frustrating for the Dean over those years to see the non-existent choir popping up on most Sundays and even during the week as well!
>
> The fact is of course that the media saw Mr Jensen's two greatest faults as being the Archbishop's brother (heaven forbid!) and having a penchant for preaching the Bible directly and unashamedly. Adding to that such crimes as the use of a communion table that could be moved...there was no stopping some journalists from adding whatever false information suited them.
>
> The Dean has given fine gospel service at the Cathedral and the organist and choirmaster continues to do so. And yes, folks, there really is a choir.

That ends the letters to papers aspect of this book, but I would add a few contributions that I made to "Column 8" in *The Sydney Morning Herald* over some time. The column was originally the last column on the front page of the newspaper when it first began in 1947 and has been mentioned earlier with regard to Auntie Cath's early contribution with her letter to George Bernard Shaw. When the number of columns on the page changed it retained its title. Column 8 started with the signature "Granny" at the bottom and it was often called "Granny's column" by my mother and others. For some years the "Granny" ascription disappeared but some years ago it re-appeared. Years ago it was removed from the front page and now lives five days a week (once six) on the same page as the letters to the editor. Here are some of the ninety or more pieces of mine that have been published in that column.

8th January, 2004

"Did you notice," asks David Morrison, of Springwood, "that Tuesday's highest rainfall was at Deepwater and the lowest temperature was at Perisher?"

19th August, 2008

"The sign telling people to 'Use reciprocals provided' is obviously a joke," insists David Morrison of Springwood. "They're just trying to put one over you." You've gotta love a silly maths joke, doncha?

3rd February, 2010

On boat names, David Morrison, of Springwood, heard of an Anglican minister who had a small boat which he named *The Parish*. "If the bishop rang while he was boating, his wife could say: "I'm sorry; he's out in *The Parish*." A former travel agent, Brian Harvey of Dubbo, had a client with a cruiser moored in Sydney which he had named *The Office*.

23rd February, 2010

"I thought it was obvious", writes David Morrison of Springwood. "Airlines don't like passengers conjugating in galley areas because they don't want any accidence". [Understood by those who have studied inflected languages]

10th May, 2010

"Please tell your journalist colleagues," asks David Morrison of Springwood, "that students sit down to do tests. They sit for them. They do not sit tests. They do not sit down tests or sit tests down. They sit FOR tests". OK, David- we're hearing you.

30th December, 2010

For the record, the redoubtable Dabid Morrison, of Springwood, sets us all straight: "All Column 8 readers should be reminded that 'begging the question' is the English translation of <u>petitio principii</u>, which refers to using the conclusion of an argument as part of the argument.

5th April, 2014

"As a C8 PhD (awarded on February 5, 2008, I believe that David Morrison has contributed enough to be granted a C8PhD by publication," recommends Michael Sparkes of Braddon. "This is a major achievement in the academic world, and I don't see why it shouldn't be for Column 8 as well." We concur. Arise, Dr David, C8PhD!

[I think that is what is known as a dis-honorary doctorate.]

Auntie Margaret and the DC3

Elsewhere in this miscellany of words there is a photo of one of the DC3 aeroplanes that took passengers from Sydney to Goodooga and to four or five other places on the way. (If you are asking where Goodooga is, you have skipped a few pages!). While I was there teaching my father's brother's sister, Margaret Morrison, Auntie Margaret, decided to take the plane trip and stay with her brother who had a property some way out of town. She had to try to pick a dry period because if there was heavy rain no one would have been able to come into town and pick her up. The dirt road would be unusable by the only available vehicles. But of course if it rained heavily before the plane arrived it would be not be able to land and take off anyway.

On her way home, while in the air, she noticed that one of the two propellers was not turning. The story as I heard it was that she asked the hostess (as women flight attendants were called in those days) why the propeller wasn't turning. The hostess replied that she would ask the pilot. When the hostess returned she said that all was OK; it was just that that engine had stopped working and the pilot had "feathered" the propeller- that is, stopped it turning so that it would not be a drag on the plane. The pilot of course put the plane down as soon as possible and the passengers had to wait some hours until a replacement plane arrived. More than once Auntie's brother and his wife, or his son and her wife, invited us out to the sheep property for a meal, as did other property owners from time to time.

Teaching Music

Before I went to Goodooga I had had nearly four years of piano lessons and about two of organ lessons. That didn't make me a great musician but it did enable me to use my music skills to help out in the small town, in the school, in church services and at town events such as the ANZAC day service and Carols by Candlelight. One father in the town and one grandmother on a property asked me if I would be willing to teach the piano to their son and granddaughter, respectively.

The only piano available at first was in the small town hall and I taught the two (separately) after school. Later we bought a piano for the school, after the grandmother had bought a new one for her granddaughter and after I had spent an hour or two or three of my holidays looking at instruments in a Sydney music shop on behalf of the grandmother. Both the father of one music student and the grandmother of the other- Mr Frost the bank manager and Mrs O'Keefe on the sheep property- were themselves pianists but apparently they thought someone else would be more appropriate as a teacher.

When the school finally bought a piano we were able to do more with music. In my final year at Goodooga I found a short children's operetta and after much practice and rehearsal we were able to put on a show for the town. It was part of an evening in the local hall and it was the main attraction. Some men of the town put the school piano on the back of a truck and transported it to the hall. I'm thankful to say that the move didn't put it out of tune, as such moves often do! I conducted from the piano. At the end of the piano introduction the curtain opened and just as the chorus was about to sing, the sight of the costumes brought a loud and long round of applause from the audience. It wasn't only the Man Who Claps First, but I'm sure he started it. My back was to the audience and so he got away with it.

Fortunately the choir didn't try to sing above the applause and when it was quiet again I simply went back to the beginning and played the introduction again. At the end of the performance David Maher, the Principal ("Headmaster" in those days) asked if the audience would like to hear some parts again and when someone said "all of it" we set to and did it all over again. It lasted only about thirty minutes, perhaps a bit less, and everyone seemed to enjoy the encore. When we visited the school in 2010 David Maher suggested I sit at the piano and play some of the operetta accompaniments for old times' sake, a good idea, but the instrument was almost unplayable. The school facilities and provision of staff were almost unbelievably better than they were in 1963, but the lack of a decent piano was clearly a minus in any evaluation of the place.

The Manly Ferry

It appears that Manly, the Sydney suburb, was so named because the first Governor of New South Wales, Captain Arthur Phillip, considered the Aboriginal men he saw there to be fine physical examples of manhood. My first memories of Manly are actually of the journey there by ferry from Circular Quay at the southern extremity of Sydney's Central Business District. The ferries in those days were steam-driven, powered by coal or oil. It was always a thrill to look down into the engine room and see a big cylinder going back and forth. The smell of hot metal sticks in the memory.

Another feature that sticks in the memory was the presence of a man playing a violin for our entertainment and for his benefit as people gave him a coin or two (which were worth a lot more than similar coins today). There must have been more than one violinist playing at any one as more than one ferry would be on the go. The last such musician was, I think, playing sometime in the 1970s.

The history of successive Manly ferries is an interesting one. The ferries I remember as a boy and until I was in my early forties were around 1,200 tonnes and included the *Barragoola*, the *Dee Why* and the *Curl Curl*, as well as the slighter larger *South Steyne*. These ferries were at first all steam-powered and I believe they were built in Scotland in the 1920s and 1930s. They came from Scotland to Australia under their own steam and were retired from service in the early 1980s.

When a heavy swell was rolling at the harbour Heads there was always promise of an exciting ride. Many people of course then and now have used the ferry service as a daily way of getting to work. Stephen and I have memories of an exciting ride in about 1978.

In 1945 my uncle, my mother's brother, Clive Bayliss, returned from his years as a prisoner-of-war. He came home in the Hospital ship *Wanganella* and his family must have found out that the ship would be moored in Sydney Harbour near the Heads. From memory, several of us, including Clive's wife Lorna and his brother Charles, my brother and sister and I, and maybe one or two others such as Clive's son Paul, travelled to Manly on the ferry in order to see the *Wanganella*. We had a very big piece of cardboard or paper with "Clive Bayliss" written on it. As we passed the ship we held the sheet out but Clive told us later that he didn't see it. I suppose it was the thought that counted. It must have been an emotional time for the adults present in the group. As I recall, Clive had no hard feelings towards the Japanese in the following years, but his mother found it very hard to forgive them.

> A journalist: "There's a rumour in Canberra..."
> Menzies: "I'm sure there is".
> Menzies (at another time): "I'll bet each of these conflicting allegations about me comes from an 'unimpeachable source'".
> Menzies said he was once told that one couldn't get into trouble for what one didn't say. He later commented, "There's a great deal of truth in that, though in my experience what you don't say is frequently reported".

The author at Circular Quay in Sydney ca 1943

Look whom they're accepting now!

It was in 2017. I took a bus from Heidelberg Railway Station in Melbourne. It was a bus trip that involved a big circle around Melbourne suburbs and it took a considerable time. The service went both ways and since I was travelling about a quarter of the way it was vital to catch the right one. After checking with the driver there was no problem.

The day was a reminder of a time in about 2004 that I planned to take a circle bus in Brisbane. It would stop very near my destination but a transport official at a bus station told me that it would be silly to take that bus. Take such and such a bus, he said, and you will get their much sooner. I did- and I didn't. I ended up getting a taxi at the place from where that bus terminated and arrived at least an hour later than planned.

But back to my story. The Melbourne bus carried me to the aged care facility at Box Hill where the aged widow of a cousin of mine was living. Early in my visit my cousin and I were standing in a large lounge room, talking, and the only other people in the room were two elderly ladies, both apparently residents. I noticed one the ladies looking at me in a disapproving way and then I heard her say "They're letting in any Tom, Dick and Harry these days". The other lady assured her that I was simply a visitor. And as well as letting me in they also let me out.

Batteries for sitting on

During my first trip to New Zealand, in late 1967 and early 1968, our tour group was in Rotorua for two or three nights. On one night we went to the local hall where some Maoris were putting on a special performance for tourists and anyone else interested. It was interesting to me that most of the performers were like me surnamed Morrison, not exactly an indigenous Maori name. When we arrived we were told that the hall was overbooked and would two or three of us mind watching the show from the wings. That of course meant being right up there with the players, especially when they were coming and going from the wings to the stage and back. Their last performance involved dancing the haka. One of the men suddenly grabbed me and "persuaded" me to go on to the stage, about three or four metres from where I was standing, in full view of the audience. He gave a very quick lesson and there I was dancing the haka along with the experts. If you are still alive when you read this ask me for a demonstration. If not alive, be thankful. That is, if I'm still alive and you are too.

While in Rotorua seven of us decided to take a plane ride to see some of the sights from the air. The pilot said there were only six seats and one of us would have to sit on the battery. That one turned out to be the author of this book. The battery had a small cushion for comfort but there was no seatbelt. We saw some very interesting features, the most impressive one being the Tarawera crater which resulted from a big volcanic eruption in the nineteenth century. Many people were killed in that event. As for the battery, I can't help wondering how its use fitted into air safety regulations. But it left me with an interesting memory!

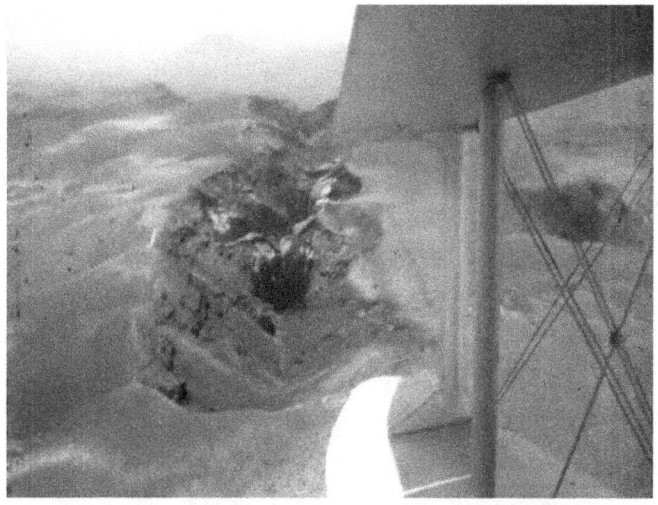

The Tarawera Crater in 1967, photographed from the battery

Uncle Joe and Auntie Flo

My grandfather's sister, Florence ("Flo") Bayliss married a man called Joe McGarry relatively late in life. Joe was thus a relatively late relative, but by the time I was sentient Uncle Joe and Auntie Flo were an established couple on a small farm at Orton Park, a township on the railway line just west of Bathurst. There was a railway station there at the time, but I think it ceased being used by the 1960s. When we visited them there in the 1940s and 50s we were struck by the almost derelict look of their home. In one room the ceiling was partly falling down, hanging there until one day it would surely drop to the floor.

On one trip I remember my mother helping Auntie Flo in the kitchen while we children waited outside in a shed where we were going to eat. I can't remember what was on the menu, but my mother told me afterwards that if we had seen it being prepared we wouldn't have eaten it. But I have lived to 86 so far.

I remember going for a ride on Uncle Joe's dray and when I was about six I had a ride in his "sulky", a small horse-drawn open-topped vehicle. It could take three or four adults. Over the creek and the road and the railway line was the home of other relatives, named McPhillamy. In 1953 my grandmother, mother and I spent a week in a hotel in Bathurst, visiting relatives who were still alive (We would hardly visit the other ones). On one occasion we visited

Left- my grandparents, James and Margaret Morrison

Right- Uncle Clive and my maternal grandparents, Lilian and Rudolph Bayliss

My father, far right; his brother Arthur and sisters Flora, Millie and Cath ca 1910?

Joe and Flo and then went across to the other home which we called "the McPhillamy" mansion. A relative called Lurline McPhillamy, by then a widow, was in residence and three or four others were staying there.

One aspect of the house that intrigued me was the large shutters on the downstairs windows, being perhaps ten or fifteen centimetres thick. They had been designed in the nineteenth century to keep out bushrangers and by 1953 they were more of a curiosity than a necessity. The Joe and Flo "house" has long since gone but the mansion can be seen on the right when travelling west on the main western railway line.

The McPhillamy family at one time owned the whole of Mt Panorama where the car racing track is now located. When we crossed the creek near auntie Flo's place to visit Mrs McPhillamy we came to the side of the creek with one pair of gum boots to enable us to cross the shallow water with dry feet. I crossed first and then threw the boots back for the next person. When the three of us were over I threw them back to Auntie Flo and we went on our way to the Mansion. I assume we caught a taxi to and from Orton Park that day, but my memory isn't *that* good!

A Bird at Goodooga

Mrs Gunn handled the airline bookings at Goodooga. Since there were only two flights per week at the service peak, with usually one to five passengers going as far as Goodooga on the five or six hop flight, the task was not onerous. On the other hand, when I was booked to take my first flight ever, from Goodooga in fact, the plane was unable to land at Goodooga because the dirt runway was too wet. There were two or three of us booked to Sydney and Mr Gunn drove us to Collarenebri to catch the plane. On the way we were bogged only once on the dirt road and we made it in plenty of time. The distance from one town to the other is now estimated at 185 kilometres, but I think we took a shorter route of about 150 kilometres. That covers one bird, the Douglas DC3.

Now for the other bird. One afternoon after school I am my colleague Ross Walkley walked to The Gunn's house with the purpose of buying tickets for the end of term. We knocked on the door and a distant voice rang out, "Who is it"? I called out that we were Ross and David and The Voice said "What do want?" "We want to book plane seats" I cried. Again the voice said "Who is it? What do you want"? After a couple more attempts to communicate I suddenly doubled up with laughter and Ross thought I had gone a bit crazy. He hadn't yet realised that no one was at home and we were conversing with a bird. I thought it was a cockatoo, but one of the Gunn's daughters told me in an email about sixty years later that it was a galah. At the time I felt that we were the galahs.

In 1964 some of our family attended a liberal Party meeting in Hornsby, a northern suburb of Sydney, with the attraction for us that the Prime Minister, Sir Robert Menzies, was the main speaker. At the time the Democratic Labor Party was recommending that DLP voters give their second preferences to the Liberal or Country Parties and they thus helped keep Labor out of office for many years. A lady in the audience kept calling out "What about the DLP, the Dirty Little Prawns?" He ignored her for a bit until she shouted very loudly "The Dirty Little Prawns, Mr Menzies!" The rather tall and corpulent Prime Minister stopped and then said "Madam, did you call me a dirty little prawn? I object to the word 'little' ". I don't think that bit of repartee was noticed by most of the audience and thus hasn't gone down in history. You read it first here, folks.

Papyrus and Adolf Deissman

What does papyrus, used in antiquity, I hear you cry, have to do with life as I have seen it? Just a very little bit. When I was studying Greek from 2003 to 2008 the main lecturer was Professor Greg Horsely at the University of New England in Armidale, New South Wales. He was particularly interested, among other things, in ancient documents and inscriptions, especially those in Greek. Part of our Greek study involved looking at copies of papyri and translating them into English. The original documents of the New Testament, as with the originals of almost all ancient literature, are not now to be found. We have to rely on copies of copies of copies, which differ from one an another in many mostly minor details, and the extensive work done by textual critics to determine as far as possible what the originals said exactly.

One important fact to keep in mind is that we have far more copies of New Testament documents than of most other ancient literary documents. In addition, the earliest copies we have (called the earliest "extant" copies) are much closer in time to the originals- usually by centuries- than the works of Homer, Plato, Aristotle for example. The documents we looked at were not those classed as literature and they were originals. They included such things as letters from soldiers to those at home and lists of items for various purposes. The main purpose of studying them was to see if they helped in understanding words and phrases used in the New Testament.

To cut short what could be a very long story, even from my very limited knowledge of the subject, my best memory is holding in my hand a piece of papyrus from the third or fourth centuries AD. It was a portion of the ancient Greek version of the Old Testament, known as the Septuagint or LXX for short. It was protected by thin sheets of Perspex, was two-sided and had been in the possession of Adolf Deissman, a German who was known to some as the "father of modern papyrology". Professor Horsely was at one stage visiting the son of Deissman, who was then in his old age. The son said that his father had left something in a drawer and asked if Greg Horsely would like it. Of course he would! To me it was a great thrill to handle the precious item.

The Patons

John Paton was a sergeant in the Indian Mutiny in the middle of the nineteenth century. He was awarded the Victoria Cross for bravery, not long after Queen Victoria had started the award. He also served in the Crimean War before moving to Australia and working as Governor of the Goulburn Gaol until he retired to Summer Hill, now very much an inner suburb of Sydney. He and his wife had two daughters known as Tina and Bella, both of whom had died as elderly ladies by 1950. The daughters never married and once they had passed on there were no living descendants. I remember them well. They left their house and all their goods to various members of the Morrison family. The main interest here is that the dining room table and chairs that we have had throughout our married life are from their home. I assume they date back to very early in the twentieth century or even a bit earlier.

My Pruen Connection with Edward Jenner, *or* Sir Henry Parkes meets Grandma, *or* Avuncular Vaccinations

Connection? None really, since Parkes died over forty years before I was born and Jenner died long before that. My maternal grandmother, Lilian May Pruen at the time (later married to Watty Rudolph Bayliss) told me that she had met Sir Henry Parkes at some kind of reception. Grandma must have been in her late teens because Sir Henry died when she was twenty. He is known as the Father of Federation as an acknowledgement of his part in bringing the colonies of the Australian continent to join as a federation in 1901. He died nearly five years before it happened, but his work was vital in helping in bringing the change about.

That surname, Pruen, has at least one amusing occurrence attached to it. It is a French name and had the unfortunate fate that it was pronounced "prune" by Australians, including my grandmother. When her brother, Edward Jenner Pruen, joined the army in World War I he avoided being ribbed by his future colleagues by enlisting as Edward Jenner. And why did he have the names Edward Jenner as his two given names? Because, dear reader, of his side of the family being almost descended from Edward Jenner, the man (mentioned earlier) who discovered the best kind of smallpox vaccination. I call my smallpox vaccination an avuncular vaccination because, as mentioned before, he was our uncle several greats removed, if I can out it that way. And "avuncular" means something to do with uncles.

The Photography Exhibition and the Talent Quest

The only occasion in my life (and so let the world be thankful) when I was called on to judge a photographic competition was in 1962 or 1963 in the small town hall in Goodooga. A teaching colleague and I agreed to judge the photos and thus please a few photographers and displease others. Our technical knowledge of the good and bad aspect of photos was slight and we didn't see eye to eye, or lens to lens, on some photographic points. At least I think we may have agreed enough to prevent a complete disaster of judgement. We did our best and the best photos won- so long as you accept that by definition the best photos are the photos that we chose. My memory is also vaguely aware of an art competition that we also judged, but the fact that the memory is vague is probably significant, if the event did actually happen.

As for the talent quest- my appointment on the grand occasion was to the role of pianist to provide background music where desired. The trouble was that the only "popular" music sheet was one particular song (I have forgotten what it was) and I played it over and over, with whatever variations I could muster (and I wasn't much good at improvising). Somehow I survived. My accompaniment was mostly needed when there was a sensible or silly dance that someone was attempting to perform. Good fun was had by all. I was much more confident at carols by candle-light and ANZAC day services where traditional hymns and carols and national songs were the order of the day (or night).

The Old Hotel at Dubbo

Are you still reading? Good for you! In 1997 I had retired and an early delight at that time was to take some train trips knowing that when I arrived home I would not have to go back to work. There was a ticket that enabled me to travel economy class anywhere on country routes in the state for two weeks. One trip was to Dubbo where I stayed overnight in a cheap hotel with a big breakfast included in the tariff. My room was old and shabby but it was big and had its own bathroom. The floors were thin and being above the bar area the noise of patrons talking loudly came up through the floor as a loud murmur. When I went out into the corridor to look for dinner the sound from below was even more pronounced. It was as though there were a thousand ghosts chattering behind all the walls. It was a slightly unnerving experience.

I had dinner in the dining room of the hotel and listened to country and western music as we ate. I love the words of country and western songs such as "Bury me back on the prairie, but first make sure that I'm dead". That isn't an actual song I've heard, but you get the idea. Some words of such songs are really funny. It was a good meal and I had some good conversation with a real Australian or two. That night I retired to my bed but not to sleep.

The sounds coming up through the floor continued until about one in the morning when the last drinker apparently left the building or went to bed. At last I was able to sleep, at least until about three o'clock when some kind of very loud operation began to take place near the railway line a hundred or so metres away. By breakfast time I had had maybe three hours sleep and was too tired to enjoy the big meal that was available in the dining room. By the way, "had had" brings to mind an attempt to use as many "hads" in a row as possible. The number is limitless, but one example might be "the man who wrote "had had' had had 'had had', had he not? And so on. Lots of fun can be had with words if one is of the right disposition!

George Henry

George Henry, mentioned earlier, was my father's father's sister's son. He and his wife, along with his parents, lived in Ceylon which of course has long since been called Sri Lanka. The family ran a tea plantation but George became known for his work as an artist and amateur ornithologist, one who studies birds. He produced a book called *Birds of Ceylon* and it includes a large number of colour plates of his paintings of birds as well as many of his black and white drawings. He lived in England in his retirement years and we saw him only a couple of times in his old age.

On one of the two occasions when George visited us in Springwood I and our young sons Matthew and Stephen drove up to meet him at Katoomba as he stepped off the train from Sydney. He was keen to see the picturesque Blue Mountains valleys in the dissected landscape. It was too bad that Katoomba was putting on one of its heavy mist displays and as we looked out over the valleys all we could see was a great whiteness. In fact all we could see was within maybe fifty metres of our faces.

I found one incident that day somewhat amusing. Because of the weather we went indoors to a small museum run by a man who was a bit of an authority on various things, including the deadly funnel-web spider. He was a naturalist and someone- George or I- mentioned that George had an interest in the birds of Sri Lanka, formerly called Ceylon. The museum owner proudly showed us an interesting book or booklet on the birds of Ceylon. George looked at it and said "I co-authored that."

George was a Baptist and he and his brothers and sisters were an interesting example of religious and philosophic diversity. One brother, Jim, was I think an atheist or agnostic and for a time lived in a cave just south of Sydney. He was for a time the custodian of the Macleay Museum at the University of Sydney. Another brother worked at the Mt Stromlo Observatory near Canberra and he was what is known as a spiritualist. One sister was an Anglican nun and another sister, Blanche, was a Christian Scientist, so-called. In their time I met only George, Jim and Blanche, all very personable people.

On another occasion his son Bruce and Bruce's wife drove with me to Katoomba and Bruce, also an artist, mainly of landscapes, was very impressed by the views and the King Parrots which there in numbers. King Parrots of course also grace us with their presence in Springwood. Those tame birds are very happy to take a little nourishment when we put out some seed. If we are not quick they will sit on our arms until we feed them. Rosellas also come and one often whistles for his supper on the windowsill.

The First Fleet

Our family can't compete with indigenous people for length of time in Australia, but for those who migrated here since 1788 it is interesting to look back and see how early our forebears arrived here. On my mother's side we go back to the 1788 First Fleet (a woman convict) and the 1790 Second Fleet (a soldier). Those first two fleets are usually graced with capital letters but later arrivals are just plain fleets, or more likely, individual ships. But read on.

Some Family Detail from Uncle Charlie

In this conglomeration of facts and pseudo-facts and observations I will now give a quotation from Charles Bayliss, my mother's elder brother, taken from a much longer account of his family history. His predecessors from his grandparents and beyond are of course our family as well as his. This quotation adds to some of the family history. I have edited it slightly (I have to admit that in case you see the original copy (!) sometime, as I hope you will if you are a descendant).

"My great-great-grandfather [therefore *my* great-great-great!], Joseph Baylis [one 's' then], arrived in 1790 as a member of the NSW Corps, in the *Surprise*, a ship of the Second Fleet. He remained a soldier until 1832, becoming a sergeant in 1832. In the meantime, he was granted twenty-five acres of land at Field of Mars, now the Ryde area, in 1796, and 150 acres on the Hawkesbury, near Windsor, in 1803. He appears to have, in 1824, conducted the first inn to be established at Penrith, *The Depot*. After his wife died he moved to Bathurst as a military pensioner. His sons, William and John, had moved to Bathurst where they had been employed by Thomas Kite. They were granted land south of Bathurst in about 1830. His two daughters, Sarah and Jane, had also moved to Bathurst, where Sarah had married Thomas Kite in 1820.

Joseph had died at Bathurst in 1855, aged 86, but was buried with full military honours in St Matthew's churchyard in Windsor [and his gravestone is still there]."

We also have an ancestor lady on the Bayliss side who came on the First Fleet as a convict, as mentioned. As far as I know we don't have any indigenous blood in us from either the Bayliss or Morrison side. Otherwise we would claim to go back many centuries indeed! My father's grandparents, by the way, came to Australia from Scotland.

The Mass Media

The term "mass media" was originally applied mainly to radio, television, newspaper and magazines. They now include all the stuff that enriches or infests the internet and finds its way to "phones" which do far more than the original telephones which by definition simply transmit sounds long distances. A medium of course is something that connects, such as a newspaper connecting a reader to a what a journalists has written. My purpose in mentioning the media here is to remind readers of the huge changes that those of my age have seen in our lifetime.

I am here reminded of a story our back neighbour told me many years ago. Radio was first used very early in the twentieth century. A family at about that time was sitting in a lounge room and one person read out a snippet that said that a message had been sent over a longish distance without the use of wires. Old Uncle sitting in the corner said "What nonsense!". The idea of wireless communication was too much for his comprehension.

I grew up very much aware of radio. We had a "wireless", as we called it, in the lounge room, and no other such device in the house. It had three nobs- for tuning, volume and tone and the only on/off switch was the power point at the wall. We would often sit near the radio as a family and listen to programmes, especially in the evening. There is reference to this radio in an earlier part of my story.

Apart from test transmissions, general television transmission began in Australia in 1956. The first station was Channel 9 in Sydney. At first television sets were very expensive and of course black and white and quite primitive compared to what we have today. Channel 7 and Channel 2 (the ABC) soon followed and for some years, until Channel 10 appeared, we had just three channels to choose from. In Sydney there were eight AM radio stations. FM was still years away in 1956.

There was no way of recording TV programmes and no videotapes or DVDs available - they had yet to be invented. One aspect of life that is different from today, especially before television, was that people would often say "Did you hear the Bob Dyer show last night?" and there was a good chance that the person had. Now the diversity of what different people have watched or listened to in the past twenty-four hours is huge. We have lost part of our common culture. Bob Dyer was the master quiz master and a popular rival on another station was Jack Davey.

Reel-to-reel videotapes came into use around 1970. They were black and white and were rather cumbersome to use, as were reel-to-reel audio tapes which were about to be mostly superseded by cassette tapes, which are still used by some people in 2025. About a decade later video cassettes were becoming common and of course they were eventually overtaken by DVDs, which even as I write this are looked upon by some as quite old-fashioned! I am including a mention of these things because as I look back the changes that have occurred in my lifetime are enough to set my brain reeling (or reel-to-reeling).

An amusing and uplifting programme called Old People's Home for Four-Year Olds was telecast by the ABC in about 2020 and repeated in 2022. These young children spent some hours per day over several days (not necessarily consecutive) at a home for old people whose ages ranged from the seventies to the nineties. To me one of the most amusing bits was when a four-year-old boy was asked what happened when an old person nears the end of his or her life. That was the subject of the segment and a number of the children gave their view. As far as I remember, the young boy said that towards the end "they tear and tear and tear and then- choof!" (or is it "chuff"?).

Left Almost Alone in the Exam Room

I n think it was in 2005 that my third year, first semester, examination in Greek occurred. It was probably the hardest of my (ancient) Greek papers, involving grammar and translation from English to Greek and Greek to English, including an "unseen" passage as well as passages from prescribed authors. The exam room in Sydney was a classroom with about thirty students, some doing two-hour papers and some three-hour papers. There were first year students of Greek doing a three-hour paper and I was the only one in the room doing third year work (there were probably only about ten altogether enrolled in third year).

It was a paper that required my full attention and although I heard the two-hour people leave quietly and the odd three-hour student leaving early, I didn't look up. After a long time of solid work I was suddenly confronted with a voice from the front of the room saying "Mr Morrison, you have ten minutes to go". I looked up and was startled to see that I was the only examinee left in the room, with the supervisor my only companion. It was also a relief that only ten minutes of my Classics 301 ordeal remained, after all those tough assignments and all that learning. And I actually finished the exam virtually as I crossed the finish line. And I managed a to gain a Credit.

Anaesthetics

Yes, really, anaesthetics. Before reading on, pronounce "anaesthetist"- two "s" sounds please. One thing that has improved greatly since I was a boy is the experience of being "put under" with a general anaesthetic. At that stage in history of course there had for a long time been an enormous advance from a century earlier when there were virtually no general anaesthetics at all. But in my early days doctors were still using ether, a step-up from chloroform, ether being safer but less pleasant for the patient. A mask with an absorbent pad in it would be put over the mouth and nose and liquid ether would be prayed on to the pad. The patient would be breathing a mixture of air and ether fumes and it took about thirty seconds to reach unconsciousness. I had three of those before I was eleven and the experience was very unpleasant.

When I was twelve my mother had a major operation and by that time had come the use of sodium pentothal which was injected into the arm and caused a much better experience of being put to sleep. The waking up experience was also better than with good old ether. My last general anaesthetic (so far) was when I was nineteen and I was able to have the greatly improved experience of pentothal as opposed to ether. Gas is also used along with the injection, but my point is made. Be thankful for medical advances!

Paper! Paper!

In the days of long ago when country trains had windows that opened- some still had them until about forty years ago - workmen along the line, known as fettlers, often took advantage of the slowness of the train as it moved past their work site. As passengers sat in the carriage they would the cry "Paper! Paper!". Those then in the know knew that the men wanted newspapers to read, since they were often in camps where it was not possible to buy a daily paper. There were of course no mobile phones on which to keep up with the news. I can remember as a boy hearing the cry and throwing out a paper or two. With air-conditioned trains now it would hardly be possible to throw papers out, even if there were any in the carriage to throw out.

Another custom of train travel used to be that of leaving a finished newspaper on the seat when getting off the train so that another passenger could read it. Doing that today would cause people to object to passengers leaving litter on the train. Times change.

An American man of some importance somewhere somehow, whom I watched on television decades ago, was talking about the Corn Belt in the United States where vast acreages (or hectarages) of maize are grown. Much of the grain is used to feed stock. The man in question spoke of the surplus that is often left over after harvest and said that some enterprising company had found a way of turning the grain "into cardboard". They then, he said, called it "cornflakes" and sold it as breakfast food.

So Young

Back in the 1960s when I was a teacher at St Ives North Public School there was a boy in my Fourth Class (Year 4) who was a bit of a "pain" at times. On one occasion his mother came to meet me and see why her son seemed to have problems getting along with me. He had told me his mother was coming and let me know that he expected her to give me a bit of a lecture on how best to relate to her son. The lady arrived during a lesson and I went to the classroom door to greet her. When she saw me she asked for Mr Morrison and when I said she was talking to him she appeared to be taken aback for a moment. Then she exclaimed something akin to "But you're so young! Don't let the class upset you" and she continued in that vein until she left, perhaps a little shaken. I had the impression that her son must have told her that his teacher was a silly crochety old man. At least the "old" part was wrong!

School Discipline in days of yore

It can be hard for people born late last century or in this one to realise how strict and even painful discipline methods were in years gone by. When I was in Year 2 in 1947 Mrs Brown would sometimes stand boys (but not girls) in front of the blackboard (which was black in those days) and have us doing "sums" with chalk. As we made mistakes she would hit us on the back of the legs with a cane. And that wasn't even for misbehaviour! The cane wasn't given much in the schools I attended but some schools at that time had very painful discipline regimes. I'm sure most of us were not in any way damaged by our occasional appointment with "the stick" but in the wisdom of the New South Wales Government physical punishment in public schools was banned from about 1988.

When I was teaching at Goodooga we had an evening talent quest in the local hall. As two of us teachers were leaving, after helping tidy up and thus almost the very last to leave, a teenage student threatened my colleague rather seriously. We managed to get away and the next morning the incident was reported to the headmaster. He thought it was serious enough to tell the local policeman. The policemen said he would come to the school and wanted the offending student to be in the headmaster's office. When the policeman arrived he asked the headmaster to get his cane and give the boy three "cuts" as we called them on each hand. The student was then instructed to go and apologise to the teacher concerned. While we were there the boy didn't try the same thing again.

> Sir William Joynson Hicks in the House of Commons: I see my right honourable friend shakes his head, but I am only expressing my own opinion.
> Churchill: And I am only shaking my own head.

The Milkman

Until some time in the 1950s it was normal for milk to be delivered by horse and cart. Until I was fifteen the milk was raw dairy milk, that is, not pasteurised, and was poured into a container we left at the front fence or near the front door. Mr Whibley was our milkman and his family had a dairy with real live cows less than a kilometre from us. I was in the same class as his son Henry and when he visited once a week to collect our payment for the milk he had a particular interest in us. When I was very young I remember the milkman coming twice a day, that being understandable because the cows were milked twice a day, but it was a lot of work for the milkman to milk cows and deliver twice a day.

Mr Whibley sometimes could be heard loudly giving orders to the horse as he walked from house to house delivering milk. He was fond of yelling "Get up!" to give the horse the clear message that it was time to move a bit further along the road. One morning I was lying in my bed on the verandah and my brother Robert had just come out to tell me that it was time to get up. Just at that moment the milkman shouted "Get up" and we both laughed at the coincidence. When I was fifteen the delivery suddenly changed to bottled milk as the days of the local dairy with its cows had come to an end.

The Baker

Our bread was also delivered by horse and cart until sometime in the 1950s. On at least one occasion my sister and I sat on the cart seat for a while as the baker (as we called him- he was more a deliverer of bread) walked from house to house with his large bread basket filled with white and brown loaves. We loved to meet him at the top of the steps, especially if we could say "One white and half a brown. That's the way to London town". I suspect our mother thought we were being a bit flippant, but I think the baker enjoyed it. We did.

The Village Store

About 300 or 400 metres from our house in Wahroonga was a shop called The Village Store. It was a grocery shop of the old kind where the grocer or his assistant was behind the counter and we read out the items on our list. Biscuits were in large tins and when we asked for a certain weight of a particular biscuit Mr Horne or one of his men would take biscuits out of the large tin and put them into a paper bag before weighing them on the scales. Some products were in a basement and it meant a climb up and down for the shopkeeper whenever a customer asked for something that was stored down there. There was a shop assistant, Mr Hanson, who used to give a free biscuit to children who came to the shop.

On one afternoon per week Mr Hanson would visit our house as he did his rounds taking weekly orders. My mother would read out her list while Mr H wrote down the items. The next afternoon another man would arrive in a small van and bring in the week's goodies which he would stack on a table in our back room. He would then take the box with him to be filled again for another delivery. In the days when many households had no car the delivery of milk, bread, groceries and sometimes other goods saved a lot of heavy shopping on foot. Vegetables, fruit and meat were generally bought at the shopping centre- the part of the street dedicated to shops-from the appropriate shop.

There were no supermarkets with the wide range of goods found today, but even today of course there are still many separate butchers, fruit and vegetable shops, newsagents and so on. I hope it stays that way.

> There is an old story which I think is basically a true one. It's about the Barwon River at Walgett, a somewhat remote town in north-western New South Wales. In the days when there was a train service to Walgett someone who lived there would bet a passenger that he would be unable to throw a stone across the river. He made it clear that the river was not very wide at that point and the bet was often taken. When the train arrived the local man and the "new boy" went to the bank of the river so that the test could take place. OK. Time to throw the stone. "Throw it now!" was the summons. The new man would bend down to pick up a stone and found that there was no stone or even pebble in sight. Just alluvial soil.

Ice

Many households had no refrigerator in the years immediately after the Second World War (or before it!). The alternative was an ice chest, a sort of large cabinet with room for a big ice block in the cavity at the top. Ice was delivered twice a week by the iceman. Underneath was a space set out much like the food space in a refrigerator, with no freezer compartment of course. The ice chest kept things comparatively cool but nothing frozen could be stored there. If we bought ice cream it had to be brought straight home and consumed almost immediately. We often bought an ice cream in a cone and ate it wherever we happened to be. At one stage a single scoop cost three pence ("thrippence"), about one dollar at 2025 values.

As mentioned earlier, Auntie Cath had lent my father the money to buy our house. The interest rate was cheap and in the end she forgave the balance of the debt. The dear aunt was very generous with the money she had earned as a self-taught accountant and one thing she (or was it my grandmother?) gave our family was a refrigerator in the early 1950s. The brand was Silent Knight, a kind of pun on the fact that it had no motor. The electric motors of most brands were often very noisy in those days and one thing you didn't have if you slept anywhere near the kitchen was a silent night.

The refrigerator was "powered" (don't ask me how) by a small lit gas jet underneath it. Some models, such as the one we had in Goodooga, had a kerosene flame. The Silent Knight was not very good at staying cold in summer and on very hot days it was no use hoping that anything in the very small freezer compartment would stay frozen. We teachers found that especially true in Goodooga where the maximum temperature could be above forty degrees for days at a time with minimums of twenty-five or more.

Mother's Day

My father told me that Uncle Arthur (you've met him earlier) and another man brought the idea of Mother's Day to Australia from the United States just after the First World War. As with my father, our uncle returned from the war *via* the United States- why, I have forgotten. Other people have also claimed to have brought Mother's Day to Australia and this tale is to be taken with a pinch of salt, although my father was fairly adamant that he was correct. The two men were members of Burwood Presbyterian Church and at first it was just a local remembrance. The original idea, at least with Arthur and his friend, was to wear a white flower in honour of one's own mother, whether she were alive or not and whether or not one knew the identity of one's birth mother. Adopted and foster children of course honoured the mother they knew best as well perhaps as their birth mother.

Freedom

For a change of pace the subject of freedom will be taken up at this spot. There has been a good deal of talk over the years about freedoms, including freedom of religion and freedom of expression, freedom of association and so on. My contention has been that sometimes these freedoms are falsely separated rather than keeping our eyes on freedom in general. No one of course should be "free' to do or say just anything, no matter how injurious to others, but the line between freedom and restraint has to be drawn very carefully and with liberal principles in mind.

In 1973 and 1974 the Whitlam Government had a Human Rights Bill ready to be debated and perhaps passed in both Houses of Parliament. To the minds of many of us it posed great risks to freedom, especially religious freedom. It was put forward by the Attorney-General, Senator Lionel Murphy, who was also the Leader of the Government in the Senate. Indeed he was the same Lionel Murphy with whom a couple of us had a long conversation in Goodooga back in 1963 and the same man who briefly came into my classroom the next morning.

I wrote about the Bill to our local member, a member of the Labor Party which was then in government, and to Senator Sir Kenneth Anderson, leader of the Opposition in the Senate, and whose daughter incidentally was married to a second cousin of mine. Both men, one Labor and one Liberal, agreed with me. The Bill never came anywhere near being passed. There was an unexpected double dissolution election in May 1974 and as far as I know the Bill lapsed and was never introduced again. Murphy left Parliament early in 1975 and became a Justice of the High Court, a controversial appointment at the time.

As one example of many letters ("representations") I sent to politicians over the years the following letter might be of interest. The letters was sent to Senator Anderson in February 1974.

> Dear Sir,
>
> I would like to make two points regarding the Human Rights Bill. 1973. These are put here very briefly in order to indicate that I and others of my acquaintance have some concern over some aspects of the Bill, not least being a remarkable omission. First, it seems strange that Section 4 of Article 18 of the International Covenant has been omitted from the Bill. It is to be hoped that this was merely an unfortunate mistaken omission.
>
> Secondly, Subsection 4 of Section 10 could be used in future for sinister purposes by opponents of religion or particular religions.
>
> Public comment by various bodies and individuals has emphasised the great concern by a large number of electors regarding these matters and others. I trust that this letter may add some slight weight as the Bill is debated in the Senate.
>
> There was a young bard of Japan who wrote verses that no one could scan;
> When asked for a reason, he replied in due season,

"It's because I always try to fit as many words into the last line as I possibly can".

Petticoat Government

Back in 1952, when Queen Elizabeth II had just ascended the Throne on the death of her father, we were on one occasion having afternoon tea at the house of the aunties next door. My father commented that we were now under "petticoat government" and Auntie Cath pointed out that great things had been accomplished during the reigns of female monarchs. When we look at the great strides made in all sorts of ways during the reigns of Elizabeth I, Victoria and now Elizabeth II, Auntie Cath seemed to be right about the first two and her expectations were certainly fulfilled with the third. It has occurred to me though that while those three ladies were great monarchs, and may well have been better than most English Kings, it is perhaps a little unfair to make a straight comparison when it comes to twentieth century monarchs.

There were in the twentieth century four kings, with an average reign of thirteen years. If we exclude Edward VIII, whose reign was very brief, that still gives an average of seventeen years. Elizabeth I reigned for forty-four years, Victoria for sixty-three and Elizabeth II for seventy years. Some Kings of earlier centuries had long reigns, the longest being that of George III at fifty-nine years. He was mad for a time and while he gained the Australian colonies he lost the colonies in what is now the United States of America. I'll leave to historians further comments on accomplishments of monarchs and their subjects.

Never Fear

Once when in my twenties I was at home at home in Wahroonga my mother and I espied a policeman walking up the front path. We immediately thought that a member of the family, probably my sister Wendy who also lived there, had been involved in an accident. We braced ourselves for what the police officer might be about to tell us. There was no need for alarm. We went to the door and he said something to the effect of "It's very embarrassing. I've run out of petrol. May I please use your phone?" We didn't ask him of course, but we wondered if he had been pursing another car when the fuel had run out. Since he was driving a Mini Minor he probably wasn't.

Pulpits of sand

Sometimes what is preached from a pulpit or read from a lectern is based on solid rock and sometimes on sand. Words and collections of words can be airy-fairy and like flummery or they can be like good nourishing food for the mind or the spirit, or both. But that is not what I mean to write about at this spot. What comes to my memory is the construction of sand pulpits in the days of long ago when I was involved with summer beach missions. At our main morning meeting on the beach we would sing and pray and the main part of the event was a Bible talk for the children gathered in front of us. Anyone of any age was welcome to sit and listen or stand a little way off and stand and listen.

To make the people on the stage more visible and to help project the sounds of voice and musical instrument the men on the team would get out soon after breakfast with spades and shovels and construct a sand pulpit ready for the morning meeting. The mound of sand designated by the term "pulpit" was a metre or more high and perhaps three or four metres long. It had to be wide enough from front to back to enable a few people to stand safely on it if we were doing a bit of drama, for example.

A beach mission meeting led from the sand pulpit

A Trip not Taken

In 1969 I was doing a university year-long unit on Education and a lecturer decided to organise a trip to India to look at some educational institutions there. Twenty mostly mature-age students submitted their names for the trip and I was among them. As told earlier, my smallpox vaccination for the trip made me very ill, but before I could have the other "needles" I received a letter from the lecturer saying that of the twenty people who had originally booked for the trip, eighteen had pulled out. That meant the end of the idea and as it happened I have never been in the northern hemisphere. But while I am on India, I'll tell an anecdote about nearby Sri Lanka, once called Ceylon.

The Elephant not in the Room

Auntie Flora told me this one and I believe it to be true. The Henry family told her that on one occasion in (Ceylon) Sri Lanka there were some working elephants being used by men on some sort of construction or other work near a river. At one stage some people stepped into a boat and rowed to the opposite bank, leaving their dog to swim over. For some reason the dog wouldn't go into the water but stood on the bank barking. After a short time an elephant lumbered down to the water's edge, picked up the dog with its trunk and threw the dog into the water. The dog then swam to the other shore. I suppose that is a confirmation of the reputed intelligence of elephants.

Sir Owen Dixon

Sir Owen Dixon was the Chief Justice of the High Court of Australia from 1952 to 1964. I never met him or saw him but in about 1958, when I was a clerk at the Arbitration Commission, I was asked to proof-read the type-out of one of his judgements. Another clerk and I did the job and the thing that struck me was that the document would go on for a page or more without punctuation. In other words, just like the punishments some lower judges handed out, he liked very long sentences.

On another occasion I picked up the phone and a voice said "This is Mr Justice McTiernan". I could have said "Hello Eddie" but of course I probably said something like "Yes, Your Honour?" Anyway, he wanted to know how to get hold of "Exhibit A" or Exhibit something or other and I couldn't help him until I had enquired of my boss. Sometimes I think it would have been good to stay working in that kind of environment but if I hadn't become a teacher I wouldn't have met Anna at a teacher's conference! I'm not sorry, and not only for that reason.

Blackboards

What better way for a teacher from the "olden days" to have a word about blackboards as the book nears its end? It is more accurate to call them "chalkboards" because at least in New South Wales public schools the official policy was to change them into green boards. That began to happen in the early 1950s. I remember a man coming into our high school classroom in about 1953 and while the teacher continued teaching us the man painted the blackboard green. Many teachers were still calling them blackboards when I finished full-time teaching at the end of 1996. White boards were by then proliferating and I was glad that I never had a classroom without a blackboard, even if it was nearly always green. I can't imagine trying to teach geography without a box of coloured chalk and a chalkboard.

One little bit of the history of our kindred has to do with the names of two people connected by marriage to the Morrison family. There was a Mr Down and he asked Miss Downes for her hand in marriage. She agreed not only to the hand but to the whole deal of a life together. Relatives must have had to think a bit when they acquired a Down-Downes marriage- are we going to a function at the Downs' (or the Downs's) or at the Downes' (or the Downes's)? Fortunately for the sake of non-confusion the next generation Miss Down became a Morrison

Mr and Mrs David Morrison on 1st January, 1972

Final Anecdotes

Bee- Beatrice Miles, who preferred to be called (and spelt) Bee was an eccentric lady who was best known in my time a person who frequently stopped the trams and other vehicles. My first memory of her was when my parents and siblings and I were waiting for a tram on the corner of King and George Streets in Sydney. The traffic suddenly stopped and the policemen on point duty had a big smile on his face. Then I saw a rather burly looking woman jump on and off the running boards of trams and swing her haversack round as she ran from one tram to another. Bee was what used to be known as an "identity" in Sydney, unmistakable because of the clothes she wore. Our family saw her at various times, always peaceful times apart from that first occasion. The closest I came to meeting Bee was an occasion when some of us family members were sitting in a café and Bee borrowed a pen from my father in order to complete the crossword puzzle in the newspaper. I was amazed at how rapidly she filled in the answers to the clues. By the way, running boards on trams might not be familiar to many readers, but a digression on trams will have to wait for another book.

Four teachers- It was interesting to observe while teaching in Goodooga how we four teachers formed an almost unique team for those days in the early 1960s. We were all male, all non-smokers and all notionally Protestants. This is a chance for me to sneak in a bit of pedantry about the word "unique". The word means that there is and ever was only one of its kind in existence. Thus something can be almost unique but it can't be said to be very unique. It's unique or it's not. Like this book isn't. But a bit of pedantry is one way to fill a paragraph.

Penny-farthings- My one attempt to ride a penny-farthing bicycle happened in the late 1950s or early 60s. Riding it was fairly easy so long as it was mounted from something above ground level. The difficulty was dismounting, which I accomplished by falling sideways. That is not to be recommended. Don't try it at home, as the saying goes. There is a right way to mount and dismount as I saw on television over sixty years later. The penny-farthing is still used by enthusiasts but it was already out of regular use by almost everyone long before I was born. Those bicycles get their name from the use of a very large front wheel and a very small back wheel. The farthing was a coin worth one quarter of a penny, a coin out of use by the time I arrived in the world. Pennies were still part of our currency until we changed to decimal currency on the "fourteenth of February, 1966", to quote words from a song that was used to get us ready for the change.

Bad beer- As a mostly non-drinker I would be unable to comment on whether a particular batch of beer was good or not, but there was an occasion where I found the discussion mildly amusing. I had played the organ for a wedding in Hebel in southern Queensland and we had then sat ourselves down for the reception feast under temporary cover next to the church building. There was abundant beer, from a barrel I think, and most of the guests soon got drinking (or imbibing, as some would say). As time passed there were various comments long the lines of "this beer isn't very good. I hope it improves". Many of those present made sure they didn't give up too early in the hope that the next glass would be better than the previous one.

Rations- One great thing happened on my sixth birthday in 1945, about five months before the war finished. Soon after that birthday with a cake with white icing (coloured icing was banned, as was ice cream that wasn't vanilla- wartime restrictions you know) my parents and I were at the spot in Wahroonga town centre where ration coupons were being handed out. In those days and for some years after the war there was rationing of various items such as tea, sugar, butter and petrol. On this occasion the man at the table pointed out that now I was six I was eligible for a regular ration of tea. I felt important at being old enough for a tea ration and I am sure my parents were the ones who benefited in practice. Britain had much more severe food shortages during and after the war and we were encouraged to donate tins of food to be sent for distribution there. The British plight was of course not nearly as bad as it was in some countries such as the occupied Netherlands where my wife was an infant in the latter part of the war.

Dentists- If space were unlimited I could tell of dentists good and bad, the bad being the one who took out several of my juvenile teeth under two general anaesthetics (administered by a doctor) during my very early years. Several of the subsequent permanent teeth grew crookedly and my tooth life thereafter was one of great interest and even a challenge to the dentists who took me on. There was the incompetent or neglectful one who dealt with my mouth during my teens, the top dentist in Macquarie Street Sydney who took an hour and a half to extract a tooth when I was about 20, and finally two dentists who took me on in early middle age and dealt with me until there was no further need of a dentist. The names of those two are Graham Toulmin and Roger Phillips.

Graham interrupted his work years in Australia when he and his family went to Africa as a missionary family while he and his wife Wendy went to the Democratic Republic of the Congo again for a few years when the children had grown up. Both Roger and Graham put up with my supposed sense of humour, such as when I reminded them of the old saying "You be true to your teeth and they'll never be false to you". I mention those two especially because they didn't just me make me a connoisseur of block injections and the various ways of using a probe. I have known them both in church and other contexts and have valued their friendship and fellowship. And they never made me feel down in the mouth.

Mosquitos- Goodooga had a very generous ration of Australia's mosquitos. When I lived in the hotel I used a mosquito net over the bed almost every night of the year, with a small electric fan in summer blowing air on to me through the net to assuage the often stifling heat of the night. There was a story that the mosquitos of Goodooga were so big that they could lift a person up. Apparently on one occasion two large insects lifted a man up, one at the head and the other at the foot. Without warning the one at the foot dropped him and the one at the other end said "Why did you do that?" The one at the foot replied that it was better to eat the man there and then. Otherwise if they carried him home the big ones would eat him.

That story no doubt belongs to the genre of Australian short stories known as "tall stories", such as the tales about the Speewah, a mythical sheep station. But that's another story for another book.

...

Perhaps that is enough. I could go on about the joy of having three flavours of ice cream available some time after the war finished, the fact that very tall buildings were banned in Sydney until the 1960s, the cute sayings of our children when very young (without names attached!) and so on and so on. If you happen to be family members you might be interested to delve further into family history. Information can be found in various places such as photo albums, copies of family trees, historical notes and the like. My overall aim has been to give some information about me and my side of the family, as well as my observations on a few of the things that have happened in the world in my lifetime. Children of the twenty-first century have I hope been interested in what life was like in the twentieth. The most important aspect of my life has of course been my Christian faith and it is my hope and prayer that as many readers as possible will also be able to say that now or in the future.

The second most important has been my marriage to a wonderful lady. Close on the heels of that are our five children and twelve grandchildren. My parents and my brother and sister must also come in for special mention. And if you have read thus far, whether you are a relative or friend or acquaintance or simply an interested reader, thank you for being longsuffering. I have made little or no mention of our children and grandchildren in the book because in the main the biographical parts of the story are designed to give them some account of family history on my side, most or much of which is from before their time. The book is for them, not about them.

Maybe I should have begun the book twenty or more years ago before the wells of creativity were so intent on drying up, but that can't be remedied now.

Farewell.

THE END

SOLI DEO GLORIA

www.ingramcontent.com/pod-product-compliance
Lightning Source LLC
Chambersburg PA
CBHW032111090426
42743CB00007B/318